Way To Go!

Way To Go!

A Chronicle of Heroes and Legends
of Bay Area Sports

by Ron Fimrite

Tarquin Books

Mill Valley, California

Acknowledgements

The following article is reprinted from *TOUCHDOWN* by permission of Touchdown Publications, Inc.
 The Rooting Section

 The following articles are reprinted by permission of the *San Francisco Chronicle*.
 The Battle of Brunk's Run, The Voices of Spring, The World's Greatest Runner, Remember the Day, Ronnie and Harvey Revisited, The Legend of Squirmin' Herman, We Wandered Today to the Game, Maggie (Copyright 1970), When Palo Alto Knew Its Place (Copyright 1970), It Was Then a Shanty Town (Copyright 1969), Who-Dat Gudat (Copyright 1970), Andy's Eulogy Still Lives (Copyright 1970), The Great Big Fast Scout Report (Copyright 1971), This is What It's All About (Copyright 1970), He Was Pappy to Us All (Copyright 1969)

 The following articles are reprinted from *Sports Illustrated* by permission of Time, Inc. Copyright 1972, 1973, 1974, 1975, 1976, 1977, 1978.
 Way to Go, Trivia, Fear of Flying, Disciples of Another Creed, Lucky Devil, He Changed a Game Singlehandedly, Send in the Clown, Cable Cars, Fog and Willie, Reggie! Reggie! Reggie!, Men Suited to a T, The Battle is Rejoined, Vintage Juice 1864, Affairs of the Heart, Football Odyssey

 Permission to reprint these articles, either whole or in part, must be obtained from the original copyright holders.

International Standard Book Number: 0-932600-00-X

Tarquin Books
530 Northern Avenue
Mill Valley, California 94941

Designed and produced by
Randolph-Harris, Incorporated
Berkeley, California

Printed and bound by Consolidated Printers, Inc.
Berkeley, California

Cover design and illustrations by Bill Thomas
Cover photo by Suzanne Stafford

Printed in the United States of America

Introduction

The pieces assembled here are all, in one form or another, about sports and the sporting life in the San Francisco Bay Area. The bulk of them were originally written for *Sports Illustrated* magazine, which employs me, of course, to write about sports anywhere it sees fit. It might seem surprising, then, that so much of what I have written for this estimable national publication should have a Bay Area orientation, particularly since many of the stories were written during the three and a half years I lived in Manhattan (before S.I. kindly allowed me to come home again). This proves, I suppose, that you can take the boy out of the Bay Area, but you can't take the Bay Area out of the boy. Quite frankly, I don't ever want the Bay Area taken out of me or me out of it again. This is home, the roots. I love it. It has long been a consuming interest of mine to explore this area's rich sports history. You will observe I say, "sports history," carefully eschewing that unfortunate word, "nostalgia," which connotes gooey sentimentality. There is sentiment on these pages—without the goo, I hope—but my real purpose has been to isolate a few moments in our past and try to breathe some life into them. For better or worse, sports are part of our passing social scene and deserve, therefore, some measure of scholarship. Think of the Twenties, for example, and, chances are, Babe Ruth's name will spring as readily to mind as Lindbergh's or Coolidge's. Sports can tell us a little about ourselves, what we are and what we were. That, humbly, is what I'm trying to do here.

In selecting these stories, publisher Les Tusup and I had to make certain, first of all, that they "held up," that they were not instantly dated. As a result, you will find few truly "news" stories on these pages, for nothing gets old faster than news. The one that does qualify as news is the account of O.J. Simpson's breaking Jim Brown's rushing record in New York, a story written on the spot under deadline circumstances. That record has "held up" pretty well, though, and O.J., like the author, is home again, so we included it.

This is not to imply that everything you read here is "timeless." Some of the columns written for *The Chronicle* are ten years old, and they refer to a slightly different type of college student than we find now. But in other ways, I think they "hold up" rather well, which says a little about progress. There have been some, shall we say, situational changes. Jackie Jensen is no longer the Cal baseball coach. He is living the life of a gentleman farmer in Virginia, but his general sense of well-being is the same now as it was when the story you read here was written. I need not point out, I'm sure, that tuition has gone up at Stanford in the past six years. And when I wrote about Trivia, it was a fairly exotic pursuit, confined largely to dark barrooms; now it appears to be a national craze. But you can still find Mel Corvin down at the Templebar. Some verities are eternal.

Writing about something you care about is, though certainly labor, a labor of love, nevertheless. I can only hope some of the pleasure I found in doing these stories about my home will translate itself to you, the indulgent reader.

— *R.F.*

Table of Contents

Way to Go, and The Way It Went

*A Series of instructive home movies featuring the
author's tight brushes with the great, near-great,
has-beens and never wases*

I had never been in greater haste to leave a place. The documents
releasing me from two years of undistinguished Army service were
in hand as I burst into the company recreation room to tender some
swift farewells.

Then, out of the corner of an eye, I saw the familiar, compelling
glimmer. It was shed by an 11-inch television screen, around which
were clustered the usual dozen or more transfixed young soldiers.
Now this was a time in my life when I could not pass a television
screen without pausing to stare hopelessly at it, be the fare *Play-
house 90* or *Sheena, Queen of the Jungle*. So even in my headlong
flight from the colors, I stopped to see what was on. It was Sept.
29, 1954, my last day in the Army, Independence Day.

Mine was not a television generation. Radio was our opium. TV had arrived too late to hold us in thrall as say, *Fibber McGee and Molly* had. It was a curiosity, although there was no arguing its hypnotic powers, its capacity for clouding men's minds. If the set was on, you watched, whether the program was a wrestling match or a cooking lesson.

What was on this day was the opening game of the 1954 World Series between the New York Giants and the Cleveland Indians. It was the eighth inning when I stopped to watch, drawn irresistibly to the shimmering eye.

And, of course, it *was* the World Series. Don Liddle—"Little Don Liddle"—was pitching for the Giants with Vic Wertz batting. Two men were on base; the score was 2-2. Wertz was a power hitter, capable of winning the game right then. I could not leave. Besides, after two years of defending Western civilization, as we know it, against the Asiatic Communist hordes from behind a typewriter in West Germany, what could a few more minutes matter?

On the next pitch, Wertz slugged the ball into the boundless reaches of center field in the Polo Grounds. Willie Mays, the Giants' young centerfielder, turned his back to home plate and set off in what was obviously futile pursuit. Mays' best hope, it seemed, was to prevent an inside-the-park home run with a quick recovery and accurate throw.

On the small, flickering screen, Mays was running, running, as if there were no walls to contain him, as if he would track down the ball even if it should descend in a Harlem alley. The ball appeared as a feathery blur, fluttering like a homing pigeon toward the running man. Mays did not even seem to look up as it nestled into his reaching glove.

The audience in the rec room exploded in celebration. We shouted, stomped our feet and punched each other in the arm, that being a popular means of expressing emotion in those days. We did not embrace, for even in our excitement we were, above all else, "cool." Mostly, we just shouted, "Way to go, Willie. Way to go!"

Broadcaster Russ Hodges advised us that we had just witnessed one of the great catches in World Series history. We could hardly dispute that judgment, since most of us had not seen so much as a routine catch in World Series history. We saw it "live," if but once, instant replay being some 10 years away. It was a good moment.

"Way to go, Willie," I chortled to myself as I hurried off to the future that lay in wait. "Way to go!"

I only dimly perceived that what I had just seen *was*, in a sense, history. I had no idea that the future I was about to embrace so ardently would include a "sports world" of staggering immensity, or that TV, that flickering screen, would capture and illuminate it so insistently.

Television may have breathed life into some sports, notably professional football, but it killed minor league baseball and mortally wounded boxing. Minor league baseball had an attendance of 42 million in 1949; in 1973 it was 11 million. In the same period, the number of teams dropped from 488 to 144. The fans had become accustomed to watching big-league games for free on TV. Boxing seemed at first to thrive on television coverage. The Wednesday- and Friday-night fights were prime-time attractions and name boxers were created overnight—Chico Vejar, Chuck Davey, Ralph (Tiger) Jones. But the constant exposure ruined the boxing clubs that had been the training ground of champions. There were 300 clubs in 1952, fewer than 50 only seven years later. Then televised boxing reached the limbo of overexposure. By the end of the decade, save for the high-priced theater broadcasts, boxing had all but vanished from the air.

* * *

The Richmond Auditorium across the bay from San Francisco was a tidy, greenish building, not at all like the decaying, smoke-filled arenas of fight-game legend. High school basketball seemed more appropriate to these congenial surroundings and, indeed, when the boxing crowd was not there that was the auditorium's principal attraction. And yet the Richmond fight club was successful in the 50s and, like the others, it cultivated its own crop of local favorites. The one I will always remember was Eddie Machen, a heavyweight who later became a leading contender.

Machen was the king of Richmond in the mid-50s, a powerfully muscled, handsome black man with the air of a champion. His clothes—gaudy, brilliant, luminous combinations—were at least 10 years in advance of male fashion. He was seldom without a dazzling beauty on his arm, and his arrival in the Richmond Auditorium would invariably signal a standing ovation.

Machen would later be knocked out by Ingemar Johansson, then an unknown, and he would take a terrible beating from Floyd Patterson. Finally, he would suffer a nervous breakdown, be embarrassed by several bizarre altercations with the police (one involving a gun) and, at the age of 40, a broken, sad wreck of a man, he would die mysteriously from a fall off his apartment deck in San Francisco's Mission District.

I cannot say for certain if Machen was in the auditorium on April 10, 1956, the night I saw Archie Moore fight there. He probably was, for in those days he seldom missed an opportunity to be introduced in the Richmond ring. But even if he had been there he would have been overshadowed, since it was rare for the local promoters to book a celebrity of Moore's stature. Moore was still the light heavyweight champion of the world, and only seven months earlier he had fought a gallant heavyweight title match with Rocky Marciano before succumbing in the ninth round. But he had knocked the champion down early in the fight and he remained a champion in his own right. The knowledgeable fight fans in Richmond flocked in great numbers—maybe 3,000—to see this venerable warrior meet an obscure local heavyweight, one Willie Bean.

I was covering the fight for the *Berkeley Gazette*. I say "covering," although that is not an accurate description of what I was doing, since boxing was a beat I had created for myself. I had been hired away by the *Gazette* from a public-relations job—for which I was monumentally unsuited—to cover high school sports in the East Bay. Boxing was definitely not part of that assignment. The *Gazette*, a parochial college-town paper then, had ignored the sport, presumably in the belief, later confirmed, that it would go away. Boxing also happened to be just one of many sports of which the then sports editor knew nothing and cared less.

As a fight fan, I felt the *Gazette* had been derelict in eschewing the Richmond matches, and I was determined to compensate personally for that neglect. So I appeared at ringside every week, utilizing credentials that had once been passed on to typographers.

I was there, as usual, to see Moore's Richmond debut. Actually, I had seen him fight eight years before in Oakland, when he had lost in a single round to a local hopeful, Leonard Morrow. This brief encounter raised many eyebrows, since Morrow was young and promising, a potential contender, and Moore, who had already been fighting a dozen years, was in the trial-horse period of his career. Rumors, always unfounded, persisted that the older combatant had been handsomely compensated for excusing himself early from the hostilities.

But in 1956 that seemed long ago. Moore's career had recently taken a dramatic turn upward at a time when it might have been expected to wind down. He had become a champion in the 50s. He had fought and defeated the best light heavies and many of the heavies. He had achieved a reputation as a mystic through an Australian aborigine diet that allowed him to fight one night weighing more than 200 pounds and only a few months later at the light-heavyweight limit of 175. He was the wily and respected elder statesman of the squared circle. He was The Mongoose.

Moore looked less mystic than bored as he labored through the ropes into the Richmond ring. He wore a richly brocaded robe that, nonetheless, seemed faded. When he removed it, his belly was revealed, fairly spilling over the waistband of trunks that were so long they looked like Bermuda shorts. He weighed nearly 25 pounds more than he had for the Marciano fight and he carried this excess poorly. He was hardly a figure to inspire awe, a fat, graying, middle-aged man of either 43 or 40, depending on whether one accepted the birth date he faithfully recited or the earlier one his mother inadvertently disclosed during an interview. Only the long, thick boxer's arms were impressive.

Bean, Moore's opponent, was more athletic looking. He was tall and flat-bellied, with wide shoulders and a thick neck. The muscles on his back rippled as he danced, face lowered, in his corner. But when he turned to confront the portly old party opposite him, it was apparent he was scared stiff. He had never before fought any-one as formidable as Moore. He was a tune-up, and he knew it. He was already perspiring heavily. He was finished before he started.

He was, in fact, finished not long after he started. Moore cuffed him at will in the first two rounds, puffing from the exertion. The Mongoose was annoyed that his prey would not come to him, that he was obliged to plod after the frightened wretch. Bean scarcely threw a punch. His eyes were wide with apprehension.

In the fifth round Moore reached him with a combination of pon-derous blows. Bean folded up along the ropes above me, not so much injured as relieved, even grateful, to have the ordeal come to a close. Moore consented to have his arm raised, then he hurried from the ring, the great tummy bouncing beneath the robe.

We writers also rushed to the dressing room, although I was detained by officious functionaries demanding to see my press pass. Did I look so callow they could not recognized me as a certified fight writer?

By the time I reached Moore's dressing room the other reporters were leaving it. Apparently Moore had not had much to say about the lackluster confrontation. I plunged into the room and found myself alone with the great man, save for a trainer off in one corner stirring his elixirs.

Moore was supine on the rubbing table, absolutely motionless. His eyes were closed. A Johnny Hodges solo on, as I recall, *I Got It Bad and That Ain't Good* reached us from a record player near Moore's place of rest. I started to say something like "Hi, Archie," but before I could utter a syllable, he raised a hand to silence me. The alto sax had more to say to him at that moment.

I was then—and am, regrettably, now—uncomfortable in the presence of athletes in a locker room. It is their place of business, and though it is obviously also mine, I cannot help but feel like an interloper. Perhaps I was too long a fan before I troubled to talk to famous athletes. Although in some company I am considered glib—even, at certain hours of the evening, garrulous—around athletes I am without conversational resources. I am often resentful of my tongue-tied inability to say anything remotely intelligent to even the most unlettered lout of a game player. It is, I suppose, a hang-up.

So, on this night, I sat in a chair as Moore lay there like a corpse. The two of us listened wordlessly as the fine old Ellington record spun to a conclusion. Moore may well have been sound asleep when I padded embarrassedly out of the room, although I could have sworn I saw the trainer wink at him as I gently closed the door.

The next day I wrote that Moore, the cagey old Mongoose, had dispatched poor Bean with such consummate ease there was little he could say about the experience afterward. That was pretty much what the other writers wrote.

★ ★ ★

It was a different tour than it is today," said Arnold Palmer. "More camaraderie. The game was faster. There was a different breed of golfer. You knew everybody on the tour. It was not as large in numbers, but the quality of the golfers was just as good. Now, of course, there are a lot more good golfers, but the guys I was playing with were damn good. There's no question about that."

★ ★ ★

Nineteen sixty-seven was not a good year for Ken Venturi. His hands had gone numb because of some strange circulatory ailment, his marriage to a beautiful and charming women was beginning to come apart, and his younger son had been seriously injured in an auto accident. But he had won the 1964 U.S. Open and he still had money, fast cars and a big house with a swimming pool in the same town, Hillsborough, Calif., that Bing Crosby lived in. He had always been a complex man, part small boy with an easily bruised ego and a sense that the world orbited around him, part old man with a wistful feel for the past, a nagging sense of loss and a carefully structured notion of how things ought to be.

Golf is not a game I care about, but Venturi in his prime was such a craftsman it was impossible not to admire him. His swing, they say, was among the best ever. He was not particularly large or strong, but he had an athlete's grace, a way of moving that the rest of us can only envy.

I had known him casually for a number of years, mostly during a time when no one outside the San Francisco Bay Area had ever heard of him. "Ken Venturi is going to be the greatest golfer in history," a friend of his told me one night when both of us were still undergraduates. "People won't even mention Hogan's name in the same breath."

That prophecy was nearly realized. Venturi was a child prodigy, an amateur who almost won the Masters, and he had risen to glory in concert with an even more famous golfer, Arnold Palmer. His rapid descent was, in hyperbolic sports vernacular, tragic.

I saw Venturi only a month or so ago at a football game. He seemed happy, adjusted, O.K. He lives in Palm Springs now. He has a new wife, a new life and he is the friend of Frank Sinatra. The boyish charm is intact. In his 40s, Venturi still speaks in the 1950s' college idiom: people are "out to lunch" or "way out in left field."

But on a night some seven years ago, when a friend and I had dinner at his house, he was burdened by an inner torment. The life he had carefully built for himself, the happy-go-lucky professional golfer's life, was disintegrating and he had no alternative plan. We had several martinis. We recalled old friends and we spoke positively of his future. His wife, Conni, busied herself with hors d'oeuvres and drink-mixing. Venturi likes bluff male companionship.

He brought a large manilla folder into the room. "Look at these," he said, spreading some letters on the coffee table. "Here's one from Charley Johnson, the Cardinals' quarterback. A smart guy, Ph.D., the works. He says I'm an inspiration to him. Me, an inspiration? How 'bout that?"

Venturi was then entering what he hoped would be the comeback phase of his life. He had created a character for himself—the good man you can't keep down—and he was living the part. "I can grip the club now," he said. "It won't be long."

We, his guests, believed him. What was more gratifying than a comeback? Life at its best was a comeback. Destry rides again.

"You remember that cover of me on *Sports Illustrated*?" he said. "C'mon, I want to show you something."

Venturi led us into a room just off the living room. It was dark. We could see nothing. Then he flipped the light switch and one wall was brilliantly illuminated. On it was the *Sports Illustrated* cover blown up to life-size. There was Venturi in his ulitmate moment, an exhausted, exultant figure raising a white cap victoriously. We could almost share that feeling, looking at the giant reproduction. The white cap? It was like the fourth feather "Leftenant" Faversham returned to his fiancee in a movie that had shaped all of our lives— the triumphant underdog, the coward proved brave.

I do not know how long we stood there before that bright image. I could not see the expression on the real Venturi's face. I felt confused, as if there was something I should say, but I could think of nothing.

"Let's go get something to eat," he said, flipping the light switch, shutting off the glory.

✱   ✱   ✱

Baseball was the first sport to be televised, an otherwise unimportant game between Columbia and Princeton being telecast over W2XBS, New York, as early as May 17, 1939. And in the postwar years the World Series was TV's prestige sports attraction. Yet baseball, of all games, cannot be adequately portrayed on the small screen. The action is too diffuse, the players too departmentalized to be captured in a single picture. Professional football, an incipient rival in the early 50s, would reap the media harvest instead. The National Football League championship game of 1958 between the Baltimore Colts and the New York Giants would assure that sport electronic preeminence, presumably forever. In the next decade, pro football's popularity would approach mania.

✱   ✱   ✱

Of all the bartenders in San Francisco in the decade of the 60s, and their number was legion, James S. Todt did the best Bogart. His impersonation was uncannily close to the real article, and he might go an entire shift without slipping out of character. If someone in Todt's presence would advance toward the jukebox, he might grumble moodily, "You played it for her, you can play it for me." Or he might startle a woman customer by gazing disconsolately into her glass before protesting, "Of all the gin joints in all the towns in all the world, she walks into mine." Questioned on a matter of principle, Todt invariably rejoined, "Fred C. Dobbs don't say nothin' he don't mean."

But even this superb entertainer was not immune from ordinary human failings. In the opinion of Todt watchers he had one stupendous imperfection—his fanatical devotion to San Francisco 49er Quarterback John Brodie, whose career in the 60s was a masterwork of inconsistency. All starting 49er quarterbacks were mercilessly booed and their replacements extravagantly praised in those years, but none endured the abuse Brodie shouldered, for none played so long. Eventually, a fence had to be erected above the players' tunnel at Kezar Stadium to shield Brodie from those who would skull him with beer cans.

Todt's fidelity to his persecuted idol was unshakable. He had followed Brodie since the quarterback's sophomore year at Stanford, and when Brodie joined the 49ers in 1957 Todt founded the John Brodie Fan Club of Northern California, an organization he prophesied would soon surpass in both numbers and fanaticism societies formed on behalf of Elvis Presley and the late James Dean. Ten years later the JBFCNC was still in business, and Todt was able to report in his annual message to his constituents, "We have doubled our membership to five."

After several years of hearing the various Todt bon mots, of auditioning his Bogey and his Benny—"Now cut that out"—I found it hard to believe that an intelligent man in his 40s could possibly be that serious about Brodie. True, I had received messages from him on JBFCNC stationery, but that seemed simply part of the running gag.

Then one day I was invited to the Todt home to watch a 49er out-of-town game on television. Todt himself answered the door. He was wearing a 49er helmet and a red No. 12 jersey, Brodie's number. The costume was only peripherally intended to amuse. It helped Todt get in a proper frame of mind—insane—for the game. Lord, how that man suffered as his hero would first engineer a masterful drive into enemy territory, then toss the interception that terminated it. "John, John, John . . ." Todt moaned at the television screen. He nearly wept when the game ended unfavorably for the home team—if memory serves, on a Brodie interception. There was no more questioning his devotion. I felt like someone who had debunked Bernadette.

Somewhat later, I attended a game at Kezar Stadium with Todt, his wife, Judy, and some of their friends. The day began, as every 49er game began for them, in a neighborhood bar, where Todt exchanged japes and wagers with other regulars. The entire party was eventually loaded—and that *is* the word—aboard a rented bus for the trip to Golden Gate Park and the dilapidated stadium.

Most of the fans in the Todts' section had been season ticket-holders for many years. They had come to know each other well. Still, the Todts were celebrities. "Here comes big No. 12," someone shouted as Todt, mounting the steps, smiled and raised a hand in a V signal. The bench seats in the old Kezar were built for a slenderer generation of football watchers so that when the crowd exceeded 50,000 the fans were closely packed. Contiguity can breed contempt, and Todt and his seatmates were soon involved in a surprisingly hostile debate on the relative merits of Brodie and his rookie heir apparent, Steve Spurrier.

Todt nevertheless maintained his composure under fire. Mrs. Todt was experiencing a somewhat stiffer struggle with her own self-restraint. Finally, when the gentleman seated in front of Todt taunted him, in terms Mrs. Todt regarded as unconscionably personal, on a misfired Brodie pass, she shook the bottle of champagne she had been enjoying and directed the contents at the face of her husband's tormentor. The ensuing melee was typical of a Sunday afternoon in Kezar in those years of high passion. There were no arrests and only a few minor injuries.

One question remained: Had Todt ever met his idol, his John, face-to-face? I approached him on this matter one evening at a bar where he was then employed. Todt had just finished informing an astonished woman sitting next to me that "Yes, Angel, I'm gonna send you over," but he answered me in the unfamiliar voice of James S. Todt.

"Yes, I did meet John not long ago. It was in the steam room of the Ambassador Health Club. We were both naked as jaybirds, mind you. A mutual friend told John, 'Now here's a guy you just gotta meet.' John knew all about the fan club and about the trouble I usually get into because of it so he didn't say anything at first. He just looked me up and down. Then he said, 'Jim, I thought you'd look much different.' Different? I was afraid he was gonna say something like, 'I thought you'd be a much younger, thinner, better-looking guy.' 'Different in what way?' I asked. 'Well,' he said, 'I thought you'd have bruises all over your body.'

It was the start, as Rick advised Louis that eventful night at the Casablanca airport, "of a beautiful friendship."

✱ ✱ ✱

In the 1954-55 season there were eight blacks in the entire National Basketball Association. The league is now more than 60% black and five of the 18 head coaches are black. The average annual salary in the NBA is $90,000 and 25% of the players make more than $100,000.

★ ★ ★

Very few professional athletes become part of the community where they play. Nate Thurmond, when he was the center of the Warriors, did become part of San Francisco. He was seen everywhere—in the bars and restaurants, at banquets and parties, at baseball and football games. Almost no one saw Willie Mays in public, but Thurmond got around. He was single, and he lived in the city, not in some remote, self-contained suburb. He owned a restaurant in town and he was a fixture there. One day a spurned girlfriend of his deliberately crashed one of his two expensive automobiles directly into the other while it was parked in front of the restaurant. Thurmond watched the disaster from the doorway.

On another occasion he asked a sportswriter friend if he could get into a banquet. "Sure," the friend told Thurmond, who was nearly seven feet tall, black and practically bald. "Wear a red carnation so they'll be able to identify you at the door."

He lived high as the highest-paid player on the team. His apartment was supposed to be a showplace. He had girls by the score. He dressed not so much as a modern athlete—gaudy suits and such—but as a striped-suited international banker.

One night a few years ago, while we were all whooping it up at Perry's Bar on Union Street, Thurmond invited some of us over for a nightcap at his lush Russian Hill apartment. I had never been there and was anxious to go. I wanted to see how this giant poohbah lived. I liked his style.

With directions scratched on a cocktail napkin, I drove off with a friend for the nightcap. We had some trouble parking the car—almost as much as we had driving it—but we finally did locate ourselves near the building. "Nate is supposed to live on the 12th floor," I remarked to my friend in the lobby, "but this elevator only goes to the 11th."

"He lives on the roof," said my friend, attempting to sound knowledgeable through the blur of his diction. "In a penthouse."

We got out on the 11th floor and ascended a flight of stairs to the roof. It was a spectacularly clear, moonlit night. We could see the bay shimmering beneath us. What we could not see was anything resembling an apartment.

In the adjoining building, however, a party was going on in a magnificently appointed apartment. We could see through the open windows scores of pretty women, well-dressed men and all manner of food and drink. The laughter penetrated the cool, crisp night air. We watched, like two waifs pressing faces against a candy-store window. Swaying there on the roof, we were captivated by the opulence and gaiety. It was the sort of party we had always wanted to be invited to.

Then, suddenly, our view was gone, obliterated by a giant figure in front of the window. We Peeping Toms cursed his rudeness. When he finally moved away, we could see he was nearly seven feet tall, black and practically bald. He was wearing a striped suit.

"Wrong building," said my friend.

"Oh, what the hell," I said.

We watched only a few minutes more, then I drove him to his apartment and returned home to my wakening wife. "Where have you been all this time?" she asked. "Nowhere," I said.

✻ ✻ ✻

During the past 20 years Americans have steadily become a nation of participants. Inspired, perhaps, by President Kennedy's plea for physical fitness, Americans have been jogging, hiking, bicycling, skiing and playing tennis and golf. The Kennedy's set an example with their family touch-football games. Sales of sports equipment, according to a National Sporting Goods Association survey, are up more than 600% since 1955. More than 100 million Americans now swim regularly, the same number ride bicycles and 20 million play tennis. The emphasis has been on participation for its own sake as opposed to the win philosophy long espoused by the powers in big-time college and professional sport.

✻ ✻ ✻

A newspaper columnist I know wrote not long ago about how mature he had become in his approach to competitive athletics. He told how he had been such a bad loser for so many years and how, now that he was nearing 40, he had seen the light. His wife and he can play as tennis doubles partners these days without a single slurring remark about backhands or double faults. They can play, he insisted, without even caring whether they win or lose. He can leave the court, he wrote, feeling comfortable in the knowledge that he had done his best and if that had not been good enough, well then, *c'est la vie.*

Bully, I say, for him. It is just that I have not run across many people who can put this philosophy into practice, including me. What happens in real life is that when most of us turn to playing children's games—and what game is not a children's game?—we tend to behave like children. I envy my columnist friend his new-found maturity. At the same time I mourn the blandness that seems to have crept into his sporting life, such as it is. Take the infantile out of sport and you have taken the joy out of it. The playing field is an unlikely place to discover maturity. And exercising for exercising's sake is an exercise in boredom. What, after all, is so keen about being grown up? People who fall in love are not grown-up.

When I was a boy, I read somewhere that Elroy (Crazy Legs) Hirsch learned to be such a neat broken-field runner by dodging weeds and shrubbery in vacant lots. From then on, I could not pass a vacant lot without dodging through its flora crazy-leggedly. The temptation, alas, is still there, although now I content myself with walking briskly down crowded metropolitan streets, head-faking a lady shopper here, giving the hip to a messenger boy there, utilizing my "quick feet" to elude a street vendor over there, all the while giving free reign to a fevered imagination. "Fimrite has the ball on the 10, he's up to the 20, the 30. He makes a great move . . . There's only one man who can stop him now and that's the great Glenn Davis . . . He is outrunning Davis . . . He scores for California."

I was pleased, incidentally, to learn some time ago from a onetime great broken-field runner, Hugh McElhenny, that the process can be reversed. McElhenny told me that when he was dodging tacklers on NFL gridirons he imagined himself a little kid hurrying home from a scary movie. He knew there were monsters in every doorway ready to leap out at him, and though he could not see them, he would anticipate their moves and elude them instinctively.

When President Kennedy advised us all to get off our duffs and start working out, I, as a loyal Kennedy man, dutifully obliged. Jogging was both boring and painful, and I had long since abandoned golf and tennis as too hard on the nervous system, so I took up what was then known as paddleball and is now called racquetball. My physical condition has not improved much, but I have at least reached a detente with my bad habits.

I will also play a little softball from time to time, reciting, predictably, a familiar litany: "It's a fast ball high and inside. Fimrite swings and there's a long, high fly ball to deep center field. Mays goes back, but that ball is going, going, *gone*"—all that before popping up to second base.

Touch football is something else. This is a game I should definitely give up, as any number of pulled muscles and deep bruises will attest. I will not give it up, of course, simply because it affords an opportunity to indulge those childish fantasies. "The hand-off is to Fimrite . . . He's swinging wide around left end . . ." There yet remains the chance that I will cut back against the grain of taggers, pick up some blocking and "break one."

Several weeks ago I was asked to play in a game of touch with a number of men, most of whom were only slightly younger than I. Naturally, I accepted, flattered that they should think the old boy still had something left. I had a pretty good day out there, hitting on three of the four passes they allowed me to throw and intercepting another. I must confess, though, that late in the going I was overtaken by a certain inexplicable fatigue. Dead game to the last, I refused to be taken out.

About this time the other team had the ball deep in our territory and, though we were comfortably ahead, I was alert for a possible second interception. Their quarterback dropped back to pass on first down, and I could see a receiver—a sturdily built youngster still in his 20s—speeding into my zone, searching, undoubtedly for the crease. As a crafty veteran, I calculated that this late in the game they might be foolishly planning to "pick on me."

Sure enough, the quarterback spotted my man and released the ball just as I moved in for the interception. Ball, receiver and aging defender arrived simultaneously. The ball and receiver advanced a few more yards after the collision before he was necktie-tagged by another defender. I remained behind, clutching my injured head like some latter-day Y.A. Tittle, blood seeping through my fingers.

I was carted off to a hospital, where a deep eye cut was stitched. The eye itself soon closed under a mass of discolored flesh. Ali did not do so much damage to Foreman.

There were guests in my house when I returned. I instantly became a figure of ridicule and misplaced pity. "What did you say at the hospital when you gave your age and then told them how you got hurt?" one friend inquired. And was that a "No fool like an old fool" I heard in the back of the room?

"Now, just wait a minute," I said, fixing the assemblage with an icy, Cyclopean glare. "You are forgetting the most important thing, the only thing."

There was a momentary silence, as if there might be some interest in what I might say next.

"You forget," I continued, allowing a suggestion of pride to color my tone of voice, "you forget that whatever might have happened to me, whatever pain I might have endured—and you must learn to play with pain—and whatever permanent injury I may have suffered . . . we still won the game."

★   ★   ★

So 20 years have passed. There have been changes, I suppose. There are major league teams everywhere now, and most of them play not on the fields of friendly strife but on ersatz grass. But how many changes have there really been? George Blanda says that in his 26 years as a professional, football has changed hardly at all, except that the players are bigger, faster, smarter and more disloyal to their employers. He also says that the new breed of pro, the rookies fresh from college, are "more like us old guys."

Change is never apparent until a new change occurs. Anyway, change is not so much what you remember over the years. What you recall are isolated incidents, apparently meaningless events or people you cannot get out of your mind. Think of them and you pause in the mad dash into the future, pause long enough to gauge the distance you have come.

How many thousands of sports events have I seen on television since the opening game of the 1954 World Series? And yet there will always be that unforgettable catch, Mays running, running . . . running off into memory.

And when was the last time I said, "Way to go?" Why just now.

We Wandered Today to The Game, Maggie

Decided to drop by Old Frat House on Big Game Day. Be good to bridge generation gap and cut up touches with a lot of Old Guys whose names I can't recall. Besides, it's a good place to park car.

Campus always seems to look same on Big Game Day. Mainly, I suppose, because all the Old Guys come back. Like me. Old Frat House, however, has been completely rebuilt. Doesn't look cruddy anymore. Lost all its charm.

Park car on sidewalk next to Towaway Sign, knowing cops are always benevolent on Big Game Day and that guys in Old Frat House will see that nothing happens to it. Brothers in the Bonds.

★ ★ ★

Quickly notice that Frat Guys are very young. How come they let such kids into college these days? Don't recall Frat Guys being that young in My Day. Also recognize that new Frat Guys look different. Scruffy bunch. Beards and long hair. Lots of foreign-looking kids. Thought I saw guy in a burnoose.

Old Guys look same though. All clustered around beer keg. Robert Kirk sport coats with blue and gold flowers in lapels. Wives are all old. Old sorority girls. Short hair, fixed smiles. In school they never went "all the way." Now have lots of kids, which they talk about a lot.

Scruffy kid—was he in a turban?—pours me a glass of flat beer. I grunt thanks. Meet up with familiar faces. Old roommates. Brothers in Bonds. We talk about Old Days. How we used to scare each other on way to Sleeping Deck. Drinking Bouts. How we never seemed to persuade sorority girls to go "all the way."

★ ★ ★

What happened to the fish pond? World's first polluted body of water. So dark you couldn't see it, even in the daytime. Guy staggered out of Initiation Banquet one night, and all we could hear

16

is splash of water. Took four of us to fish him out.

Old Guy I recognize from Old Days joins group. Gets everybody's name wrong. He's wearing name tag. Nevertheless, one guy whose name he gets wrong purposely gets his name wrong.

Guy who used to play football walks in. He's treated by Old Guys like conquering hero. Never had too many jocks in the Old Days, so even if a guy played second string junior varsity, he was a celebrity. Always sneered at jocks until we got one. Old football player, however, doesn't join group. Seems more interested in talking to scruffy kids. Never did like jocks anyway.

★   ★   ★

Game is brief interlude in talk about Old Days, which resumes immediately after Cal whips Stanford. Fraternity Guys now bring girls into Old Frat House. Scruffy broads, but somehow . . . well . . . interesting. Probably go "all the way." Just thinking about this bothers us. Wives, the old sorority girls, get short shrift. They're talking about their kids anyway. We are ogling scruffy girls.

Old Guy comes into room with air horn. Blows it. Nobody pays any attention to him. Scruffy kids giggle. We tell him to knock it off. He looks dejected. Is obviously smashed.

Despite Great Victory in Big Game, we talk about days when Cal had Real Football Teams. Jensen, Swaner, Olszewski, Monachino, Schabarum, Richter, Ozzie Harris!

★   ★   ★

Those were guys who could really play football. Not like scruffy kids now. They had all the girls in world. Probably went "all the way" all the time. All belonged to other Frat Houses.

We decide to "look around the place," noticing that scruffy kids and their scruffy girls have left us alone by the beer keg. Go upstairs. Used to look cruddy. Now looks like Hilton Hotel. We hear funny music come out from closed doors. Oriental stuff. Rotten latin junk. Guitars. Hear female laughter. All the way?

We decide it's time to "get the hell outa here." Parties to go to with Old Sorority Girls.

It's dark outside. Cops have towed car away.

TriviaTriviaTriviaTriviaTrivia

When it is a question of competition, there are those who feel that nothing can compare with the game of minutiae, in which minor and long-forgotten characters of sport and screen and radio are the major concern

1. Since the NFL draft began, two Notre Dame quarterbacks have been the No. 1 pick. Who were they?
2. What was the name of the silent film in which John Barrymore played Captain Ahab?
3. What major league baseball player wore the name of his hometown on the back of his uniform?
4. In 1950 the American League season leader in stolen bases had just 15, the fewest in major league history. Who was he?
5. What actor played the role of the escaped prisoner who hid in the rolltop desk in the first screen version of "The Front Page"?
6. Who was the first man to coach two Heisman trophy winners?
7. Who broke Dizzy Dean's toe with a line drive in the 1937 All-Star Game? Which toe? Which foot?
8. The major league season record for most doubles is 67. Who

18

holds it?

9. What actress faced life as Portia in the radio soap opera and at the same time played Belle in "Lorenzo Jones"?

10. What was the original title of the Rodgers & Hart song "Blue Moon" when the melody was first used in the film "Manhattan Melodrama"?

11. In "One Man's Family," who played the part of Teddy?

12. Who was the catcher for the 1934 Cardinals' Gas House Gang?

13. In "Uncle Tom's Cabin," Eliza crossed a frozen river. What river was it?

14. Who were the two quarterbacks with the initials Y.A.T. who played football in Yankee Stadium?

15. Who were the twelve angry men?

16. The actress Margo is remembered for her role in "Lost Horizon." But in what film did she make her debut and who was her leading man in that movie?

17. Only one man in modern major league history ever stole six bases in one game, and he did it twice in less than two weeks. Who was he?

18. What actor played the Brazilian leading man in "Flying Down to Rio"?

19. In the seventh game of the 1946 series, Enos Slaughter, who was on first base, scored on a hit to left center field. Who hit the ball?

(Answers on page 30)

It is opening time at the Templebar in San Francisco and Mel Corvin is positioned near the kitchen, a squat, imperious figure in a dark suit of impeccable 1952 cut. Sipping coffee soundlessly, he has the wary aspect of an aging gunfighter steeling himself for the inevitable challenge. This is an image Corvin encourages, for he wishes it known that he is "trying my damnedest to phase myself out of this game." He has as much chance of achieving serenity in his time as Wild Bill Hickok had in his, and Corvin knows it. His reputation, alas, precedes him.

"It's getting so I can't walk into a place without somebody nailing me with, 'I got one for you,'" he says.

But this is merely a pose, for Corvin is not as discomfited by the prospect of somebody having one for him as he lets on. He is, after all, a trivia player, a man who welcomes—nay, embraces—challenge. And he knows further that there are only a handful of competitors in his town with the necessary grasp of arcana to extend him. Let them, then, have one for him.

If they should demand of him the batting order of the 1936 New York Yankees (a question so easy Corvin does not think it qualifies as trivia), let them try Crosetti, Rolfe, DiMaggio, Gehrig, Dickey, Powell, Lazzeri and Selkirk. If they require the actress who played Humphrey Bogart's long-suffering mother in *Dead End*, give them Marjorie Main. And if they should ask for the opening sequence of the old radio show *Grand Central Station*, he will re-create the sound of a speeding locomotive and then breathlessly announce in a voice hauntingly familiar:

"As a bullet seeks its target, shining rails in every part of our great country are aimed at Grand Central Station, heart of the nation's greatest city. Drawn by the magnetic force, the fantastic metropolis, day and night great trains rush toward the Hudson River, sweep down its eastern bank for 140 miles, flash briefly past the long, red row of tenement houses south of 125th street, dive with a roar into the 2½-mile tunnel which burrows beneath the glitter and swank of Park Avenue and then . . . Grand Central Station . . . crossroads of a million private lives."

That should hold them. But probably not for long. Indeed, while Corvin and his fellow trivialists are involved in no formal competition, they are seldom off duty. Somebody always has one for them. They are, in fact, part of a subculture group composed of persons of a certain age whose minds are hopelessly cluttered with the detritus of the Depression '30s and the warring '40s. They are, as one of their number, Tom Dunn of Albuquerque, suggests, "Forty-year-old kids singing the Jack Armstrong song." While civilization quavered before economic disaster and military threat, these kids—now, roughly, between 35 and 50—found enormous pleasure and, as it develops, lasting satisfaction out of Little Orphan Annie, Duke Mantee, Albie Booth, Ossie Bluege, Tonto and Margot Lane.

Trivia players are not to be confused with the current clutch of stowaways on the nostalgia bandwagon; the best of them have been playing the trivia game in earnest for at least 20 years, or from the time they were far enough along to look back. They are obviously in the vanguard of the backward movement.

"I'd almost burned out nostalgia on the air before it became popular," says Dunn, who occasionally livens his morning show on Albuquerque radio station KOB with excerpts from old serials and Orson Welles' *War of the Worlds*.

Trivia players regard the Johnny-come-latelies to old times with undisguised contempt. Likening the new nostalgia crowd to their distinguished company is a bit like comparing *No, No, Nanette* with *A La Recherche du Temps Perdu*. It is a question of sophistication.

A further distinction should also be made between trivia players and those who may be defined as collectors—librarianish sorts who squirrel away old magazines, pulps and baseball guides, often for resale at propitious moments. Although they are not necessarily averse to such exotica, trivia players are primarily attached to the more obvious sources of entertainment—sports, movies and radio. It is the little parts of the big things that entice them. Then, too, they are verbal people not given to rummaging in secondhand bookstores for first editions of *Detective Comics* or *Human Torch*. They are, in a sense, our oral historians.

The expression "Well, that was before my time" is totally alien to the trivia player, who will admit to nothing being before his time. As a child, he was fully as fascinated with the '20s or the '90s as he was with his own decade. He was as familiar with the exploits of T. Truxton Hare or Bugs Raymond as with those of Bruno Banducci or Bobo Newsom. But he is truest to his own period, a time when the big leagues were little and the movies were big, when radio fed the imagination, not satiated it, as television is inclined now to do.

"When we grew up," said singer Mel Tormé, a top trivia player, "the figures on the movie screen were all 25 to 50 times bigger than life. Now we look at TV, and they're all smaller than life—little guys and girls only seven inches high. At that size they just don't seem very important."

Tormé plays the game with such Hollywood chums as Mickey Rooney and Donald O'Connor, who have the melancholy distinction of being trivia figures in their own right. But most trivia enthusiasts are not celebrities. Many may be found in a neighborhood tavern, reciting ancient box scores and flawlessly identifying second leads and faces in the crowd in the old movie on the television screen back of the bar.

"How much d'ya wanna bet that's Rochelle Hudson . . . ?"

The omniscient Corvin is a San Francisco publicist who recently favored New York with his expertise while serving as an advance man for the Roller Derby. "I killed them in PJ Clarke's," he modestly acknowledges.

Trivialist Rod Belcher of Seattle, tall and red-haired, is the public information officer for the Washington Department of Highways. He is also a former radio announcer who in 1950 broadcast San Francisco 49er games under the pseudonym Rod Hughes—a deception made necessary by his sponsor's aversion to the word "belcher" when used in connection with his product, which happened to be beer. Belcher is the composer of *Go, Go, You Pilots!*, the fight song of the now-defunct American League franchise in Seattle. "We sang *Go, Go,*" said Belcher, "and they went. But the record has become a collector's item. Sales have never been better."

Trivia player Bob Hanson of Atlanta is a genial "independent insurance adjuster" who writes mocking crank letters to racist politicians and carries a business card identifying him as a purveyor of "land, whiskey, manure, nails, flyswatters, racing forms and bongos." Hanson's reputation as a trivialist is such that he is frequently called upon—usually at odd hours—to settle arguments of a familiar nature. It is Hanson, answering his bedroom phone, who will inform reveling friends downtown that Ken Maynard's horse was named Tarzan, not Topper, which, of course, was Hopalong Cassidy's steed.

Most trivia players have jobs of some sort. The New York advertising industry has a surfeit of them, and so have most newspaper offices. Other players follow even more respectable trades. Dr. James Loutzenhiser of Kansas City is a psychiatrist; Charles Moylan Jr. sits on the Baltimore City Supreme Bench; Elston Brooks is a theater critic for the Fort Worth *Star-Telegram*; E. Walker Chapman of Honolulu is the assistant general manager of the Royal Development Co., Ltd.; and Christy Schaller of Carson City, Nev. is the executive administrator to Nevada Governor Mike O'Callaghan.

This is not to suggest, however, that trivia players are necessarily men of searching intellect, despite Tormé's steadfast and self-serving assertion that "one has to have a certain erudition, a certain intellectual level, to play trivia."

Corvin, surely one of the best of the breed, has no intellectual pretensions. He is as unfamiliar with, say, Bertrand Russell's scholarship as the British philosopher-mathematician-pacifist was with Corvin's. Still, you ask yourself, could the co-author of the *Principia Mathematica* have recited the passenger manifest of the airplane hijacked to Shangri-La in *Lost Horizon*? Corvin can, and in a trice— Ronald Colman, John Howard, Edward Everett Horton, Thomas Mitchell and Isabel Jewell. Easy.

Despite their obvious advantages, trivia players are seldom intellectual bullies, unlike so many other scholars. Some weeks ago, Corvin found himself in a bar on Piedmont Avenue in Oakland. Seated next to him was a gentleman who informed him that he resided in the nearby community of Martinez.

"Oh, Joe DiMaggio's hometown," said Corvin, making what for him passes as casual conversation.

"Joe DiMaggio," said the Martinez man levelly, "was born in San Francisco."

"I'm sorry, sir," said Corvin. "Joltin' Joe, the Yankee Clipper, he with the lifetime batting average of .325, was born on November 25, 1914—I believe it was in the early afternoon—in Martinez—I'll think of the hospital in a minute."

"Wanna bet a hundred bucks on it?" the Martinez man inquired.

"Look, I don't want to take your money," said Corvin charitably. "Let's just say that if I'm wrong on any of these particulars, you win and I owe you a buck. If I'm right on all of them, you owe me a buck. Let the bartender be the judge."

Since this was an establishment frequented by sporting types whose arguments often require arbitration, the necessary reference material was available. Corvin, of course, was right on all counts.

"Buy this man a drink," the Martinez man instructed the barkeep. "He just saved me $99."

A patron in a Tacoma, Wash. tavern was not nearly so fortunate following an encounter with Belcher some years ago. Identifying himself as a Notre Dame graduate, the man noisily lamented that his alma mater had never played in a postseason bowl game (this predated the recent Cotton Bowl meetings with Texas). It was an observation guaranteed to bruise the delicate sensibilities of a trivia player of Belcher's stripe.

"Surely, my good man," he addressed the Fighting Irishman, "you forget the 1925 Rose Bowl meeting with Stanford, won, you must recall, by your old school 27-10. Elmer Layden, you will now obviously remember, scored three touchdowns that day, two on pass interceptions. Ernie Nevers, playing with both ankles injured, was a hero in defeat for Stanford. This, it must be clear to you now, was the Notre Dame team of the four Horsemen and Seven Mules. I won't even trouble you with the Horsemen, who must be as familiar to you as your own children, but just to refresh your memory, the Mules were Adam Walsh, naturally, at center, Kizer and Weibel, the guards. . . . "

"Hold on, buddy," the old grad interrupted, "I went to Notre

Dame and I can tell you. . . ."

"Miller and Back, the tackles, and Hunsinger and Collins, the ends."

"Yeah, but that game was played during the regular season. I've got $200 that says you're wrong."

Though offended by such abysmal ignorance, Belcher remained a man of scruples, and to take this blowhard's money was beneath his dignity. He merely smiled condescendingly and strode out the front door. Belcher's wife Dorothy had overheard the conversation, however, and though she hadn't the foggiest notion if Notre Dame had played in the 1925 Rose Bowl or if, in fact, the school had even fielded a team that year, she did know her husband and she also knew the Belchers were then slightly on their uppers. "I'm his wife," she blurted out, thinking of mouths to feed at home. "I'll take that bet." To Belcher's ultimate surprise, his household was $200 richer the next day.

Trivia players normally wager only sparingly, and rarely with outsiders. When a game is going—and one can start at any moment—they prefer to keep it among themselves. And since the pace is so swift, there is little time for money to change hands. Besides, betting would add an unwelcome note of venality to what is, essentially, a social occasion. Competition and companionship are reward enough, and some of the greatest games have been played only for laughs.

On one memorable day, for example, Belcher and Corvin clashed—for the first time—on Corvin's home turf, the Templebar. This was as close as trivia will ever come to a Super Bowl. Belcher recalls how the match developed:

"I was in San Francisco for a couple of days, and a friend got hold of me and said, 'There's somebody you just have to meet.' So we went into this place, and there was this guy at the end of the bar, near the kitchen. It was Corvin. Well, we started slowly enough, just casual conversation. Then we got going. I hit him with my Stanford teams—the Vow Boys and the boys before the Vow Boys. And he came back with Cal's Thunder Teams. We went all through big-league baseball, the movies and radio. I think we finally got down to the biggest stars at Presidio Junior High School. The guy's just amazing."

There are few remaining witnesses to this Game of the Decade, however, because a normal person can endure a first-rate trivia game for no more than a few minutes before he feels the need for fresh air. And trivia players, for their part, can tolerate only so many "I don't see how you guys can remember all that stuff" remarks. Two or more trivia players in one room will invariably ruin any social gathering. No one, after all, can keep up with them when they are at full throttle, and this is the sort of exclusivity that breeds cliquishness.

"Just when are those two going to stop it? Captain Midnight, indeed!"

No one, not newly published authors, not converts to militant feminism, not returning vacationers, can clear a room faster than two trivia players at the top of their form. Hostesses who have experienced such debacles have been known to grow faint at the first strains of "Wave the flag for Hudson High, boys. . . ."

Trivia players are often bewildered by these expressions of dread or hostility. Proud as they are of their own considerable gifts, they find it difficult to understand why more people are not like them. They see the ranks of the culturally deprived swollen daily by those who think of Bill Shakespeare as an Elizabethan playwright, not a Notre Dame halfback.

Astonished that so few of his listeners knew the words to the Little Orphan Annie song—"Who's that little chatterbox? The one with curly auburn locks?"—Dunn once cried out in anguish, "Where were all those people?"

Trivia player Hanson stoutly insists the best questions are those that merely revive dormant memories. He hopes fervently to elicit responses like, "Oh sure, I knew it all the time." They are usually long in coming. Hanson and Dunn are democratic trivia players, however, convinced that most people of the right age and background could perform as capably as they if only they put their minds to it. Others, notably Corvin, consider this approach demeaning and tend to move farther and farther out. Take, for example, Corvin's position on the Heisman Trophies.

"Anyone can name all the Heisman Trophy winners," he says. "A real trivia player knows who finished second and third in the voting."

Corvin regards 1946 as such a vintage Heisman year that he can name the first four finishers—Glenn Davis, Charley Trippi, Johnny Lujack and Doc Blanchard. He also knows who compiled the best three-year performance as a Heisman vote-getter Glenn Davis, who finished second in 1944, second again in 1945 and first in 1946. And the player with the next best Heisman record—Doak Walker, who was third (1947), first (1948) and third (1949).

Belcher's specialty—or hangup, if you will—is nicknames, or rather the given names of persons best known by their nicknames. The unwary will thus be confronted with Hack (Lewis) Wilson, Dixie (Fred) Walker, Jo-Jo (Joyner) White, Tuffy (Alphonse) Leemans or Arky (Joseph Floyd) Vaughan. And Belcher has disarmed many opponents by asking for the real name of Bronko Nagurski. The answer, he is always pleased to say, is Bronko. Belcher may further require a fellow player to give him the name and the academic affiliation of the loutish football player played by Dick Foran in *The Petrified Forest.* The answer, Boze Hertzlinger of Nevada Tech, is one that seldom is remembered, even by the most nimble trivialists.

The Petrified Forest is, however, a major trivia movie, as are all those in which the characters are isolated for a period of time in either a single room or a vehicle—the airplane, maybe, in *Lost Horizon,* the stagecoach in the original *Stagecoach.* A fairly simple trivia question has always been: What actor was in both the airplane and the stagecoach? The answer, as everyone knows, is Thomas Mitchell.

Animals, particularly horses and dogs, are among the trivia player's best friends. Tormé and Hanson are particularly sound in this field. Here, of course, it is considered bad form to indentify just the star's animal. The only horses worth knowing are those ridden either by a sidekick—Smiley Burnett's Ringeye— or a girl friend—Dale Evans' Buttermilk. "Get um up, Scout" is definitely for beginners.

Sidekicks, foils, bad guys and losers are trivia people. Elisha Cook Jr. is of infinitely greater worth than, say, John Carroll or James Craig. Since bigness holds little interest for him, the trivia player tends to overlook the great names of his era.

Joe DiMaggio, for example, is not a trivia person; Vince is. Don Ameche, telephone and all, is not; Jim is. Groucho, Harpo and Chico Marx are not; Zeppo and Gummo are. Judy Garland is not, neither is Deanna Durbin; Gloria Jean is. Tommy Harmon is not; Nile Kinnick is. Abbott and Costello are not; Wheeler and Woolsey are. Eddie (Rochester) Anderson is not; Mantan Moreland is. Even W.C. Fields is not truly a trivia person; his foil, Franklin Pangborn, definitely is.

The Yankees are easily the premier team of the trivia era, an honor worth automatic disqualification in the Trivia Major League. The ideal trivia team is the American League champion Detroit Tigers of 1934-35—and for no logical reason, save that they arrived in between the great Yankee teams and that their starting lineup, when read aloud, had a certain enchanting euphony: Gehringer, Greenberg, Goslin, Owen, Rowe, Rogell, Cochrane, White, Fox. Nickname freak Belcher is especially fond of this team, as well one should be of one fielding a Goose, a Freck, a Schoolboy, a Jo-Jo, a Black Mike, a Mechanical Man and, ultimately, a Flea.

The Flea happens to be the protagonist of one of Belcher's favorite trivia questions: What was the Detroit Tigers' starting lineup in the third game of the 1935 World Series? The Tiger lineup, unlike so many today, was fairly rigid then, making it an easy mark for even average trivia players. But in the '35 Series, something awful happened to it. Hank Greenberg played in only the first two games, then retired as the result of a broken wrist. So, Belcher will inquire, who played first base from the third game on? And, for that matter, who was on third? The answer is that Freck (Marv) Owen moved from third to first and little Flea (Herman) Clifton replaced him at third. It was a rare lineup change for the Tigers, and it gave Flea Clifton trivia immortality. The poor man played only 87 major league games in his career, and were it not for trivia players like Belcher he would forever remain in obscurity. The zinger part of the question is, of course, what did the Flea hit in that Series? The answer is .000—zero for 16.

Flea-type questions are always aggravating, and so are those in which the obvious answer is never correct. On a purely elementary —or low trivia—level, a favorite in this genre is: Who played Frankenstein in the original 1931 movie? A careless thinker would speedily say Boris Karloff. And he would be wrong, for Karloff played the monster. Colin Clive was Dr. Frankenstein.

Then, too, there is the multiple-layer or double-zinger question, favored by Corvin and other obscurantists. Here the player is taunted into an increasingly false sense of security. Corvin, for example, might casually inquire, "What was the name of the Green Hornet's car?" When told that it was, as we all know, the Black Beauty, Corvin will then ask, "Where did the Hornet park it?" This is a step up, but a reasonably adept trivia player will answer, "In an adjoining building." Now the zinger: "And what kind of building was it?" Even the best trivia players have foundered on this. Was it

a warehouse? An underground garage? Yankee Stadium? The mad-
dening answer is: "Supposedly abandoned."

The Hornet is a marvelous trivia person, lending himself to
endless queries. With the Hornet, a trivia player can deliver an
entire biography before he shoots the zinger. Here's an example:
Besides the fact they both wore masks, used special weapons (the
gas gun and silver bullets), had super modes of transportation (the
Black Beauty and Silver), employed sidekicks who spoke broken
English (Kato and Tonto), what else did the Green Hornet and the
Lone Ranger have in common? The answer: They were related.
Britt Reid, the Green Hornet, was the grandnephew of John Reid,
the Lone Ranger.

A classic Corvin double-zinger goes like this: Zinger (1)—Who
are the four players who have hit four home runs in one game since
1949? That's easy: Gil Hodges, Joe Adcock, Rocky Colavito and
Willie Mays. Zinger (2)—What one player was either a teammate
or an opponent of the hitter on each occasion? The answer, which
separates trivia men from trivia boys, is Billy Loes, a teammate of
Hodges on the 1950 Dodgers and of Mays on the 1961 Giants and
Adcock's foe as a Dodger in 1954 and Colavito's as an Oriole in
1959.

Perhaps the Black Beauty of all trivia questions was posed during
a lull between the first and second games of the last World Series by
Roger Angell, the New Yorker magazine writer and editor:

"You will quite naturally recall the 1949 James Cagney movie
White Heat," Angell began, innocently enough.

"To be sure."

"Then you remember, of course, that Cagney in the film had
something of a mother fixation?"

"Yes, crazy about the old girl."

"And that during a scene in the prison mess hall he noticed some
new cons at his table who looked familiar?"

"I can see them now."

"And that Cagney thinks they may have news from the outside
about mom?"

"Right on."

"So he turns to the con next to him and says, does he not? 'Ask
them: how's mom? Pass it on.'"

"Indubitably."

"And when the word reaches one of the new men, he turns and
says something like, 'Mom's dead. Pass it on.'"

"That's it exactly."

"Fine. Now my question is: Who was the third guy to pass it on?"

"Holy moley! Jeepers creepers!"

"No, Jim Thorpe."

"Why, that's it! The old athlete was then down to accepting bit parts, and if you look closely at that scene you will see his familiar flat features. Third? Who can say? But he was, indeed, passing word of mom's untimely demise on.

This is the sort of trivia question that warms the soul, joining as it does Corvinian obfuscation with the Hanson recognition principle. One experiences a sense of community with the questioner, and that is really what trivia is all about. Trivia players are forever in search of kindred spirits and shared pleasures. And they are sadly aware that their numbers are not likely to increase. "We are," as Belcher has said, "of a forgotten persuasion."

This is really the first, the last and eventually the lost trivia generation. The circumstances that spawned the trivia player can never be re-created. Depression youngsters, particularly those in small towns and cities, enjoyed pretty much the same things. They went to movies—all day on Saturday—they listened nightly to the radio and they lavished uncommon devotion on those flawless heroes of the gridiron and diamond who never smoked, drank, took dope or chased girls. "There was a time," said Dunn, "when it all seemed to fit."

There is too much now, too many things to do and see. Television, even with its *Howdy Doody* revival, is not a proper trivia instrument. The programs haven't the staying power, and there are simply too many of them. Trivia players saw the world through a smaller focus. There were 16 major league baseball teams, not 24—can anyone recite the starting lineup of the 1971 Milwaukee Brewers? Who, in fact, are they? Professional football was a piddling enterprise in the trivia player's youth. Now the sun rises and sets upon it. There were more movies then, but they were shorter and simpler. You *knew* the actors. The entire communications industry virtually exploded into being in the trivia years, and the trivia players were then able to keep up with it. Nobody can maintain that pace now.

Not long ago a trivia player was recalling for the amusement of some basically non-trivia companions what he half-seriously considered to be the best day of his life.

"It was the summer of 1938, and I was just 7," he said. "But think of it; all in one day I tasted my first marble fudge ice cream, bought the copy of *Action Comics* that introduced Superman and, to top it all off, was mistaken for Bobby Breen on a Greyhound bus. That is what I call living!"

His friends regarded him quizzically. "I've eaten marble fudge," said one. "And everybody knows Superman. But just who in the name of heaven is Bobby Breen?"

The trivia player was staggered. Are there grown-up people in this world who have not heard of Bobby Breen, the prototypical boy soprano? Am I, he thought, that isolated from the normal course of events? Am I that old?

But he finally comforted himself with the knowledge that somewhere, maybe down at the Templebar, there would be someone who would think of Bobby Breen as an old and treasured friend. Perhaps they would hoist one in the little fellow's memory. And maybe, if the mood was upon them, they would lift their voices in trembling falsetto and sing:

"Oh, there's a rainbow on the river, the skies are clearing . . ."

Trivia players have *that* going for them.

THE ANSWERS:
1. Frank (Boley) Dancewicz in 1946 and Paul Hornung, the bonus pick in 1957
2. *The Sea Beast*
3. Pitcher Bill Voiselle, who came from Ninety Six, S.C.
4. Dominic DiMaggio
5. George E. Stone
6. Ducky Pond of Yale. His Heisman winners were Larry Kelley and Clint Frank
7. Earl Averill, the Cleveland Indian outfielder. Big toe. Left foot
8. Earl Webb of the Boston Red Sox
9. Lucille Wall
10. *The Bad in Every Man*
11. Winifred Wolfe
12. Bill DeLancey
13. Ohio River
14. Y.A. Tittle, Young Arnold Tucker
15. Henry Fonda, Lee J. Cobb, Ed Begley, Jack Warden, Martin Balsam, George Voskovec, Robert Webber, Jack Klugman, Edward Binns, E.G. Marshall, Joseph Sweeney, John Fiedler
16. *Crime Without Passion*, Claude Rains

17. Eddie Collins
18. Raul Roulien
19. Harry Walker

The Battle of Brunk's Run

To some people—balding men with abdominal overhang who play dice during their lunch hours, housewives from Orinda and such who talk an awful lot about children—the USC-California football game serves only to recall The Battle of Brunk's Run.

Unfortunately, the years have decimated the ranks of this Proustian number, and newcomers to our community wallow in abysmal ignorance of this once historic occasion.

At the time, it was said that football partisans for centuries to come would recall the events of October 15, 1949.

But the game has drastically changed since then, and there is scarcely a sane man extant who could possibly express interest now in Brunk and his Run.

No, you would have had to have been there—and been there as a dedicated U.C. type—to much care. I can admit with only a trace of embarrassment that I was one of these. . . .

★   ★   ★

Both USC and Cal had teams of Rose Bowl potential that year, and their meeting on a sunny afternoon in Berkeley's Memorial Stadium drew a crowd of some 81,500.

The Berkeley campus was still swollen with returning servicemen whose primary interest was getting the hell out of school as quickly as possible and having a ball as long as they were there.

As a result, the California men's rooting section—10,000 white-shirted fanatical inebriates—had achieved fully as much celebrity as the football team.

It was known then as "The Infamous Section of Good Cheer." Largely because of its practice of departing from the traditional rah-rahs into the area of creative obscenity. A standard yell for every game was one which questioned the referee's parentage. And not all of the balloons sent on high were actually balloons.

The rooting section made the cover of a national magazine—much to that publication's embarrassment when certain

32

details of the photograph were brought to the editor's attention.

★ ★ ★

The USC game of that time was fully as important as the Big Game, and the rooters, properly equipped with vodka-soaked "Gremlin" orange juice containers, were spoiling for action.

Cal, led by the all-but-forgotten Bob Celeri and an obscure half-back named Frank Brunk, moved into an early 7 to 0 lead which seemed substantial enough, so fierce was the defensive play.

The average age of these teams, mind you, was two to three years older than that of today's College squads. For their time, they were closer to pros than amateurs.

One of the heroes, however, was a sophomore USC defensive halfback named Frank Gifford.

It was Gifford who kicked the fourth quarter field goal which, following an earlier Trojan touchdown, gave USC a seemingly sure 10-7 lead late in the game.

On the kickoff following this field goal, USC's Bob McGee kicked to Brunk.

"Brunk," the late Bill Leiser wrote at the time, "has no side-step. He doesn't dodge. He has no whirl. . . . In fact, Frank Brunk can't run."

★ ★ ★

But Brunk took that kickoff two yards deep in his end zone, headed straight up the middle of the field, shook off a tackle from the now legendary Gifford, stumbled out of another tackle near the goal and ran the whole 102 yards for a touchdown that, in effect, sent Cal to the Rose Bowl!

I wish I could tell you what happened afterward, but I was in the middle of the rooting section, and I was shoved by the exultant mob four rows forward on my face.

They say, though, that never has there been such bedlam any-where. I like to think that's true.

Fear of Flying

Jackie Jensen was the ultimate hero, an all-sports star who married a storybook girl. But the Golden Boy's world and marriage collapsed, and his shining baseball career ended in torment brought on by a dread of air travel. Today Jensen is a college coach and a changed man.

He was the Golden Boy, and never had he glittered so brightly as on his wedding day, Oct. 16, 1949. Jackie Jensen was 22 years old. He was blond and broad-shouldered; his body looked as if it had been sculpted instead of grown. He had been an All-America in football and baseball at the University of California, acclaimed as both the greatest running back in the school's history and its finest all-round athlete. Even the legend of Brick Muller and the Wonder Teams paled before his brilliance. The previous spring the Golden Boy had signed an extraordinary $75,000 contract to play baseball with the Oakland Oaks of the Pacific Coast League. Four days before the wedding he and teammate Billy Martin had been sold to the Yankees for a reported $100,000. It was a dream realized, for in a few months Jensen would be playing alongside his idol, Joe

DiMaggio, in the Yankee outfield.

Jensen's bride, Zoe Ann Olsen, shone almost as brightly as he. She was only 18, but she had won 14 national diving champion-ships and a silver medal in the 1948 Olympics. She was blonde and intelligent, and as pretty as he was handsome. The *San Francisco Chronicle* called them "the sports world's most famous sweethearts." Together they looked like a Nordic god and goddess.

Oakland motorcycle police escorted the city's favorite son and daughter from the ceremony at the First Presbyterian Church to a reception at the plush Athens Athletic Club, where they had first met. She had trained there; he had been the lifeguard. More than 1,000 persons attended the reception, including Nobel Prize-win-ning physicist Ernest O. Lawrence, songwriter Jimmy (*I'm in the Mood for Love*) McHugh, Olympic diving champion Vicki Draves, Cal Football Coach Lynn (Pappy) Waldorf, most of Jensen's Rose Bowl teammates, many of the Oaks and dozens of other nationally known sports figures.

"It was the wedding of the century," says Frank Brunk, Jensen's football teammate and fraternity brother. "They were on top and they had the whole world in front of them." "I thought the bubble would never burst," says Jensen. The young bride and groom drove off under a hailstorm of rice in a yellow Cadillac convertible toward a golden future.

✳   ✳   ✳

Late in April 1961 Zoe Ann went to the Reno railroad station to meet the *City of San Francisco* arriving from Chicago. She was there in response to a cryptic wire received at the Jensen home in nearby Lake Tahoe: CANCEL L.A. PLANS. ARRIVING ON TRAIN IN RENO. She burst into tears when her husband stepped off the train. Seen through the steam, he looked ghostly, a tired and troubled man who was old for his years. He had quit baseball the previous year at the height of his success. During six seasons as a star out-fielder with the Boston Red Sox, he had driven in more runs than anyone in the American League, including Ted Williams and Mickey Mantle. But the marriage that had begun so auspiciously was deteriorating, and as a side effect, Jensen's merely irritating fear of flying had escalated into a demoralizing phobia.

The year away from baseball had neither salvaged Jensen's marriage nor cured his neurosis. In 1961 he was trying a comeback. But a season's absence from the game had diminished his skills, and by the end of the first month he was hitting .130 with only one run batted in. He had avoided flying whenever possible—by driving 700 miles from Boston to Detroit on one occasion—but it was an exhausting regimen, and the phobia remained unconquered. The physical and mental ordeal finally had proved too arduous.

On April 29, with the Red Sox playing in Cleveland and scheduled to fly to Kansas City, Jensen bolted the team and headed west. He came to seek the ministrations of a nightclub hypnotist named Arthur Ellen, who had a reputation for succeeding where psychiatrists had failed in relieving aerophobia. Jackie and Zoe Ann drove from Reno to Las Vegas, where Ellen was closing out an engagement. After several days of hypnotic sessions, Jensen was able to rejoin the Red Sox in Los Angeles.

He finished the 1961 season, but played well below his usual standards, and hit only .263. This time he quit for good, voluntarily terminating a career that had approached brilliance. Retiring from the game did not accomplish what Jensen hoped it might. His marriage would soon fail, and the fear of flying would continue to torment him. He would experience a bewildering series of business mishaps, lose his closest friend and suffer a near-fatal illness. The golden future had turned to dust.

✶ ✶ ✶

All of us are several persons in a lifetime. The 40-year-old looks back on himself at 20 and sees a distant relation, a person whose ambitions, affections, triumphs and fears seem slightly absurd. We are never wholly what we were, nor will we remain what we are. From the vantage point of his present serenity, both the Golden Boy of 1949 and the neurotic of 1961 appear to be strangers to Jensen. He has come full cycle, back home to his university, not as a returning hero but as the baseball coach. It is a modest job, but one ideally suited to him now. Those who had been there before, who had been warmed by the glow of his achievements, are occasionally startled to see him pass by. It is as if they are seeing a ghost. Jensen is real enough, but certainly not the man he once was.

At 49 years old, he is an ardent jock grown pensive, a man of action transformed into a collector of Indian arrowheads and a student of Western history, a provincial metamorphosed into a world traveler (if only by ship), a tempestuous spouse turned doting husband to a new wife whose pursuits are intellectual, not athletic.

Dick Erickson, Jensen's teammate on California's 1948 Rose Bowl team and now an assistant chancellor of development at

Berkeley, admits that until Jensen's return in 1974, he had thought of his old teammate simply as "the most versatile athlete, the best-coordinated human being I'd ever known." The self-assured, thoughtful Jensen he sees now is a newcomer. "Why, he's a step above most people," says Erickson. "New vistas seem to have opened up for him. He has talents we never suspected he had—a great facility with language, for example. He is comfortable with people now. He was a loner then. He's no longer dependent on his athletic prowess. We are all seeing sides of Jack that we didn't know existed."

Cal Athletic Director Dave Maggard says that when he first considered hiring Jensen as baseball coach, he was surprised at the almost negative reaction he received from those who were supposedly Jensen admirers. "Nobody could tell me what he was like," Maggard says. "They'd all say he was a great athlete, and stop there. It occurred to me that for all of his fame, nobody really knew this man. Some even described him as a loser who seemed to have a knack for making a mess out of everything he got into. The negative publicity he'd had over the years had definitely tarnished that Golden Boy image."

But the more Maggard talked with Jensen, the more he was convinced that the detractors were talking about somebody else. "I had the advantage of not knowing Jack before," Maggard says. "I was pleased with what I saw. He was so open about himself, so honest. There was humility there. And pride. Loyalty is a difficult word to define, but he has it. He's loyal to the university and he's been loyal to me. He is becoming a fine teacher, and he'll be even better because he wants to be better. Jack's been through a lot, and he's been able to put himself in perspective. He has really found himself."

How odd these words must sound to those who were at Berkeley at the time of Jensen's glorious ascent. Jackie Jensen finding himself? How could he have lost what was there? In an age of heroes he was a hero supreme; he seemed to be exactly what an All-America football player was supposed to be—a clean-cut, modest Adonis with a storybook girl friend. He had an aura about him. On closer examination, all of this proved to be a facade. Jensen's lessers mistook his shyness for conceit; his idolators accepted his public humility as just another saintly virtue, not as genuine insecurity. Jensen was truly confident of what his body could do for him; after all, it had been performing athletic miracles since he was a child. He was much less sure of who he was. He had done less than find himself—he had not even started to look.

Jensen's parents were divorced when he was five. His father was the second of his mother's four husbands, and when he departed, she and her three young sons moved from San Francisco, where Jensen had been born on March 9, 1927, to Oakland. She continued working in San Francisco, commuting by ferry across the Bay six days a week to her job in a warehouse where she performed, Jensen says, "tough, man's work." She was absent from home for more than 12 hours each day, and would return in the evening too exhausted for family amenities. For Jensen it was virtually an orphan's existence, only it was much less stable. By the time he entered Oakland High School the Jensens had moved 16 times or, as Jackie puts it, "Every time the rent came due." He would spend most of the next 30 years searching for the homelife he never had, hoping to realize for his own children his childhood vision of what it must be like to have a father, a mother and a house. For such a man the breakup of a marriage can be much more than an unpleasant experience; it can represent a betrayal of principle, the defeat of a life's ambition.

By the time he reached junior high school, Jensen had acquired a surrogate father in Ralph Kerchum, his physical education teacher. Kerchum, a robust, genial outdoorsman, instantly recognized in young Jensen a wondrous athlete and a human being of unusual potential. He became Jackie's coach, counselor and lifelong friend, and Jensen has never forgotten his kindnesses.

"The fact that I had no father embarrassed me deeply," Jensen says. "I think there was more emphasis on family life then. Ralph was instrumental at a time when I needed someone. He gave me direction and self-confidence. It's funny, but when I see him today, we do the same things we did back then. We'll have a steak, go to a movie and pick up some ice cream. I'll say to him, 'Ralph, it never changes. Can't we go to a bar like other people?'"

At Oakland High School Jensen created a legend. He was twice All-City in both baseball and football and honorable mention All-City in basketball, although he played only a half season in that sport. He was the student body president, the most popular kid in town. For years, Oakland High athletes would emulate his style, his dress, his manner of speech, his distinctive floating gait.

He came to Cal after a year in the Navy, and though the football turnout of more than 230 players in 1946 was the largest in the university's history, he became an instant star. The first time he touched the ball in the season's opener against Wisconsin he returned a punt 56 yards for a touchdown. The run was a masterwork of improvisation, since Jensen's blockers barely knew who he was, let alone where he was going. "He was all over the field, dodging and leaping over guys," says Charles (Boots) Erb, a quarterback who had been Jensen's friend since both were in the fourth grade. "The rest of us just stood there on the sidelines with our mouths open. Finally somebody said, "Who in the hell is that guy?"

Jensen was selected to play in the East-West Shrine All-Star game as a freshman, a rare honor. In fact, he is the only athlete to have performed in an East-West game, a Rose Bowl, A World Series and a baseball All-Star Game. In 1947 and 1948 he became the "Golden Boy of the Golden Bears," playing both offense and defense, returning kicks, punting, passing, and most of all, dazzling everyone with his twisting, darting, shoulder-faking runs from scrimmage. At 195 pounds he was powerful and swift, but more than that, he was deceptive, a runner who, as Pappy Waldorf said, "Can elude the hand he cannot see."

He won two Big Games with Stanford—in 1947 with a pass to Halfback Paul Keckley that covered 80 yards and in 1948 with a game-saving play that Waldorf recalls as the most remarkable he has ever seen. Late in the game, with Cal leading 7-6 and Jensen back to punt on fourth and 31, the Stanford line broke through and seemed certain to block the kick. Jensen somehow evaded the charge and dodged up the middle for 32 yards and a first down. In a game against Santa Clara that year he had three runs of more than 60 yards. He ran 67 yards for a touchdown in the Rose Bowl game against Northwestern, then left in the third quarter with a leg injury. Without him Cal lost 20-14.

In 1948 Jensen averaged 7.3 yards a carry and rushed for 1,080 yards, a school ground-gaining record that survived until the 1975 season, when Chuck Muncie, carrying the ball nearly twice as often, finally broke it.

In baseball he led Cal to the first NCAA championship in 1947, compiling an earned-run average of 0.95 in league play. He was elected All-America in that sport, too. In 1949 he set a school record for home runs that lasted 25 years.

Jensen passed up his senior year to sign with the Oaks and, after less than a full season, he was sold to the Yankees. His inexperience hurt him in the big leagues, and the Yankees farmed him out to Kansas City, then traded him to Washington in 1952. Playing regularly as a Senator, Jensen honed his talents as a clutch hitter and strong-armed outfielder, but he did not achieve stardom until he was sent to the Red Sox in 1954. He hit 25 homers that season, drove in 117 runs and led the league with 22 stolen bases, a power and speed performance that compared very favorably with those of his better-known contemporaries, Mantle and Willie Mays. In 1955 Jensen tied for the league lead with 116 RBIs, and the following year he hit .315. In 1958, when he hit 35 homers and drove in a league-leading 122 runs, he was selected the American League's Most Valuable Player. Ten years after Jensen had reached the top in one sport, he reached it in another. He had played the outfield alongside both DiMaggio and Williams and still had managed to become a star in his own right. In 1959 he had another fine season, with 28 homers and 112 RBIs. Then he quit for the first time.

Although he had complained in numerous interviews that baseball was depriving him of a normal life with his wife and three children, the Red Sox and their fans were stunned by his decision. A ballplayer simply does not pack it in when he is at the top of his game. But Jensen had his reasons and, despite the public moralizing about hearth and home, those reasons involved things far more complicated than a simple longing for domesticity.

In January of 1959 Jensen was to fly east to accept an award from the Touchdown Club of Washington. He spent the hours before the flight with Erb at the Bow & Bell, a restaurant the two old friends had purchased on Oakland's Jack London Square. Erb was to accompany Jensen to Washington, join him in a round of parties in the East and nurse him through the ordeal of flying back and forth cross-country. Jensen was a troubled man that day. He had been agonizing over his marital difficulties, and he dreaded the impending flight.

Jensen had never been a heavy drinker, and despite his nervousness, had only a few beers, but his aunt had provided him with a sleeping tablet to take aboard the plane. Instead Jensen swallowed it with a beer during the drive to the San Francisco airport. He immediately suffered an attack of dizziness. At the airport he collapsed getting out of the car and had to be helped aboard the plane by Erb. Once in his seat, Jensen began shivering and sweating. A stewardess covered him with a blanket and callled the captain, who ordered him off the plane. Jensen was so embarrassed by the incident that he secreted himself that evening and for much of the next day in Erb's office at the restaurant.

It was but one of many humiliating experiences he would suffer aboard airplanes. Frank Malzone and Pete Runnels, two of his closest friends on the Red Sox, routinely hauled a semicomatose Jensen aboard team flights. "I would be out when they got me to my seat, usually with some sleeping pill," says Jensen. "Then, when the engines started, I'd be wide awake and everybody else on the plane would be sound asleep."

As a college football player Jensen had flown cross-country on several occasions. Waldorf recalls that it was he, not his star full-back, who feared air travel in those days. Major league baseball was primarily an Eastern enterprise when Jensen first signed, but some flights were made, and Jensen took them, protesting no more than any rational person with the wit to perceive that if man were meant to fly, God would have given him wings. Some of his friends date his phobia to a near-midair collision in 1954 while Jensen was traveling with an All-Star team in Japan. He was frightened at the time, but it remains only a convenient excuse, one that Jensen does not use.

Although the phobia has never been successfully treated, it has been analyzed, even to Jensen's satisfaction. Almost from the beginning the marriage of the athletic Jensens had been stormy, their mutual competitiveness exacerbating the endless rounds of accusations, jealousy and petty bickering so drearily common to mismatched couples. "It was a simple case of not being able to live with or live without each other," says the couple's longtime friend Helen Ehlers.

There is nothing terribly unusual about that condition, either. But it was complicated by the exigencies of Jensen's occupation. When their first child, a daughter named Jan, was old enough for school, Zoe Ann, who abhorred living in a strange city as the wife of a traveling ballplayer, stopped making trips to the East and remained behind in the family home at Crystal Bay on Lake Tahoe. It is a resort area, a mountain paradise for summer and winter sports, all of which Zoe Ann loved. It is also a nightclub and gambling community, and Zoe Ann loved that aspect as well.

It is one thing to fight with and worry about a wife who is with you, quite another to fight with and worry about one who is not, and the Jensens were apart for most of the year. Jensen was torn in two by his professional obligations and his anxiety over a wife who was living 3,000 miles from Boston. And because of his childhood trauma, nothing seemed more catastrophic to him than another broken home.

"Jackie's problem has never been fear of flying," hypnotist Ellen said recently. Ellen's nightclub stints are behind him, and he tends to the neuroses of several marqueesful of Hollywood stars and professional athletes. "The fear of flying is merely a subterfuge. Jackie needed the fear as an excuse to get home and patch up his marriage. Subconsciously, it developed as a good reason to leave the Red Sox and go home. He's divorced from Zoe Ann now, but he's still stuck with the fear of flying. He's protecting it, trying to prove that it's legitimate."

Ellen is not a psychiatrist, but Jensen placed more faith in his diagnostic skills than those of a number of expensive shrinks the Red Sox retained for him. He first encountered the hypnotist in 1953 at a night spot in St. Louis.

Jensen was there with Bob Oldis, a catcher with the Senators who had been having trouble with his batting. After catching the act, the ballplayers, almost as a joke, invited Ellen to use hypnosis to try to improve Oldis' hitting. Ellen hypnotized the catcher and told him that the next time he played, he would perform to the best of his ability. In his next game Oldis, a .237 career hitter, went 3 for 3. Jensen never forgot this impressive demonstration.

Ellen acknowledges that hypnosis cannot effect a permanent cure. He calls it "an important adjunct to psychiatry." Nonetheless, his "healing" powers have been publicly endorsed by the likes of Maury Wills. Jensen appears to be one of his few failures.

Jensen says he knows what is wrong with him. He feels that in time, with "Christian faith," he will be able to fly like any other person. "There is no question I was looking for an excuse to leave the ball club," he says, "and I know the fear was related to the insecurity of my first marriage. I wanted to go home, but I loved baseball. I got terribly down on myself. I could think about it rationally, ask myself why I couldn't beat this thing. 'You don't have to like flying,' I'd say to myself. 'A lot of people don't but they still fly.' But when the time came, I just couldn't make myself do it. I was using Arthur as a crutch. He's no miracle worker, but he could help me relax. Still, he couldn't make me more than I was. I came to resent myself for behaving in such an infantile way. I know I had another four years I could have played. The way I was driving in runs, I could have set some records. My only regret is that now I can't hope to be considered for the Hall of Fame."

Jensen sits in his small office in Cal's Harmon Gym. His All-

America certificates are on the wall and, wearing a Pendleton shirt and khaki trousers, the undergraduate uniform of the late '40s and early '50s, he looks much the way he must have when he was earning those honors. There are wrinkles about his eyes and mouth, but his face is still youthful, although the hair is more silver now than gold. Talking about his marriage to Zoe Ann and his phobia is painful to him, but he cannot set them aside.

"When we got married it was the beginning of a 10-year period when everything seemed to go right," he says. "I wanted a daughter and a son, and I got them. I wanted a home, and I got it. I had money. I was on top."

Zoe Ann has remarried, but she still lives in the Crystal Bay home with the youngest of the three children, Jay. Her figure is petite and athletic, but like her ex-husband's, her face is lined. She is a blackjack dealer in the Crystal Bay Club, where her garrulity, her wit and Lizabeth Scott voice clearly distinguish her from the normal run of women who work in such emporiums.

"When you're young, you always think it will never end," she says during a break from the tables. "But it always does, doesn't it? Sure, Jack and I started at the top, but we also started at the bottom like everyone else, with just ourselves." She shrugs, smiles and returns to the tables.

Jensen and Zoe Ann were married twice. She divorced him in 1963, two years after his final retirement from baseball. He moved back to San Francisco and went to work for an auto dealer who quickly went broke. Then Jensen was hospitalized with appendicitis. She visited him, and they decided to try it again. The second marriage barely survived three years. This time it was Jackie who got the divorce.

Badly shaken by this second failure at marriage, Jensen plunged with no better luck into a succession of business ventures. A promised auto dealership in Carson City, Nev. failed before it ever began. He invested in a golf course, then sold out. He worked part-time as the baseball coach at the University of Nevada and dabbled in local broadcasting. Finally, in 1966, Jensen found himself short of cash, and sold out his interest in the Bow & Bell to Erb. The transaction in all of its various and, it seems, unnecessary complexities was nearly fatal to their long friendship, which was repaired only this year.

Separated from Zoe Ann, Jensen went to work in 1967 as a TV sportscaster on KTVN in Reno. The producer of the show was a quick-witted, lively divorcee named Katharine Cortesi. A Virginian eight years younger than Jensen, she was educated in Europe, spoke several languages and was as well-traveled as he was not. For 10 years she had been an illustrator and assistant editor at *Harper's Bazaar* in New York. She had come to Reno for a divorce, had become enraptured with the mountain scenery and easygoing pace, and had decided to stay on. She and Jensen began dating. They were an unlikely pair, the down-at-the-heels has-been athlete and the cosmopolite, but they were well matched. They still are.

Katharine coaxed out Jensen's intellectual potential, exposing him to art, literature and desert exploration. More significant, she restored his courage, bolstered his flagging self-confidence and gave him a sense of proportion. In February 1968, in a ceremony performed in a ranch house by a one-armed justice of the peace, they were married. It was hardly the wedding of the century. After the ceremony the newlyweds quaffed a nuptial beer and went back to work at the television station.

Their home was the gamekeeper's cottage on a dude ranch operated by friends, in the foothills of the Sierra. Deer grazed in their backyard, coyotes howled at night, the scent of pine was pervasive. In this sylvan setting life seemed to be taking another turn in Jensen's favor.

Then, on March 26, 1969, Jensen was conducting baseball practice on the University of Nevada diamond, shouting encouragement to his mostly inept charges, when he felt a pressure in his chest. It was mild at first, then suddenly it became crushing. As the pain worsened, his arm went numb. He had one of his players drive him to the hospital in Reno. He collapsed there with a heart attack. The perfect body had broken down. Jensen was 42 years old.

He remained in the hospital for 10 days, then sailed for the Italian Riviera, where he recuperated in style at a villa belonging to Katharine's baroness aunt. After six weeks Jensen returned to the U.S. and accepted temporary work as a coach of Red Sox rookies in Jamestown, N.Y. Through he had hopes of staying in the team's minor-league system, the Sox did not offer him a permanent job. He returned to Reno, unemployed again, apprehensive anew, his health precarious, his prospects bleak. The TV deals were finished, the university could not pay him more than a pittance for coaching and he felt unwanted. "At 43 I had to start all over again," he says. "I was qualified only as a baseball man. I couldn't find a job. Katharine had to go back to work. People wouldn't believe me when I told them I was broke. Once I tried to get a job as a janitor. They laughed at me. 'Oh, c'mon Jack,' they said. 'You, Jackie Jensen, a janitor? You gotta be kidding.' I wasn't."

In 1971 he was hired by Nevada Governor Mike O'Callaghan as a deputy director in the State Office of Economic Opportunity. The job paid $12,000 a year, and Jensen was happy to take it. His troubles had left him introspective, self-analytical, aware of the strange turns fortune can take. In a relatively brief lifetime, he had been famous and forgotten, wealthy and poor, healthy and near death. He began to put the pieces together, and he discovered his problems were not unique.

"I could see that jillions of other people had gone through what I had—divorce, illness, financial struggles, starting all over. I began to think of the good times I'd had, of how lucky I had been, of all the people I had gotten to know. I began to think that people should be envious of me. At the time, we were making do with little income, but we were happy. We had the solitude, the quietness and the freshness of the desert."

He and Katharine amassed a collection of Indian artifacts. He read "everything I could get my hands on." He was enjoying life, strengthened, not weakened, by the knowledge of its ephemerality. "When you have a heart attack, you realize you won't live to be 90. You learn to be thankful for each new day," Jensen says. He began attending classes at the University of Nevada and, at 44, completed the remaining 17 units for the degree in rhetoric he had passed up at Berkeley 22 years earlier.

Then his job was phased out because of budget cutbacks, and from January to June of 1973 Jensen again found himself with little to do except indulge his new passion for reading. On June 15 his telephone rang. He set aside his book and answered. It was Maggard, inquiring if he would be interested in returning to Berkeley as baseball coach. This was the strangest twist of all, he told himself. He was being asked to go back to where it all started. He said yes.

On a brisk February day last year, the beginning of his second season as coach, the ex-Golden Boy, Cal's greatest athlete, wandered the steep slopes of the Berkeley campus wearing a sandwich board advertising BALL GAME TODAY! He bellowed the news through a blue and gold megaphone, the sound of his baritone voice halting curious students on their way to classes. There were not many that day who knew who he was, that he was not only a coach but also a legend. Jensen joined his audience in laughter. He was making a spectacle of himself, but in a good cause: promoting attendance for his baseball team. There were a few there who did remember another Jensen. This, surely, was not the same man. They were right—he was not.

"Wearing that sandwich board took more moral courage than I thought any man had," said Truck Cullom, Jensen's old teammate and friend. "I couldn't imagine someone like Jack doing it. People used to think he was aloof, conceited. Hell, how can a guy be that good, and not be conceited? The thing is, Jack never was, and he isn't now. He's just one helluva human being."

★ ★ ★

In the batting cage down the right-field line at Cal's Evans Field, a thin boy wearing glasses, shoulder-length hair, a sweat shirt, fatigue pants and, improbably, kneepads, is swinging ineffectually at baseballs propelled at him by a pitching machine. It is late afternoon, warm and clear, and the setting sun has turned nearby Harmon Gym a deep orange. Church steeples appear above the left-field fence, and the Campanile, its bells tolling for homecoming students, rises in the distance.

Jensen, wearing a blue warmup jacket and a gray road uniform, watches the young batsman. The boy is a "walk-on" candidate for his baseball team, a player of limited experience and with almost no chance of even winning a position on the junior varsity squad. And yet Jensen watches him as if he were a potential batting champion. The coach looks sturdy, ruddy. His health is good, and he is only a few pounds over his old playing weight.

"I'm not a sentimentalist," he says, "but I have such a warm feeling about being back here. It's not that people remember me. Oh, sure, some of the parents do, because I guess I was as famous then as some of the superstars are now. But the kids really don't know me. And that's the way it should be. I don't live in the past. Right now, I couldn't be happier. It's a beautiful day, and we're playing a little baseball."

The boy misses a pitch, so Jensen steps into the cage. "You've got to open up your hips and be quick with those hands, son," he says, then flicks his thick wrists. The boy, whose exposure to this professional advice will become apparent only in intramural softball games, watches gratefully as Jensen, with effortless, powerful swings, makes perfect contact. "See, no extra motion. Keep it short and sweet."

Jensen steps out of the cage, first patting the youngster on his thin shoulders. He is smiling about something. "There's an assistant coach, a young man, who maybe summed me up best," Jensen says. "He'd see me coming in from practice every day with a smile on my face, and he'd look kind of puzzled. Then one day he spoke up. 'Coach,' he said to me, 'don't you ever have bad moods?' Now, I don't know whether or not he was implying that I was an idiot for being so cheerful, but I took him seriously. Bad moods? I thought about myself and all that had happened. Bad moods? No, not now. The truth is, I just happen to think that life is pretty damn good."

When Palo Alto
Knew Its Place

I see from the television where Stanford has this great football team and everything.

Now this, like many other things happening today, is very confusing to an old Berkeley boy and inveterate Stanford-watcher. Stanford, you see, is never supposed to have a great football team, only about half of a great team. I mean, it's always supposed to be strong in the delicate positions—quarterback, for example, or wide receiver.

We of the old school like to think of Stanford football players as being more like tennis players. Tanned, blond guys who smoke pipes and can't hold their beer. We tend to overlook all those Armenians. After all, what's a big hairy guy doing at Stanford?

★ ★ ★

I know, I know. All this has changed now. All college students look alike these days—skinny kids with bare feet and hair down to the spinal column, guys who say "man" a lot and like guitar music.

Still, stereotypes die hard, and those of us who have always known what a Stanford guy is like won't let him go. We simply can't accept a football team that plays rough and wins important games. Plunkett is o.k. He doesn't look much like a Stanford guy— far too big, for one thing—but he is a quarterback, and Stanford has always had those. It's the rest of those people we can't accept.

The ideal Stanford football player was a guy like Bob Anderson. Remember him? A halfback in the late forties. Blond guy, tricky runner who got hurt easily. He was a swimmer, actually. Just went out for football for the hell of it. Now, that's a Stanford guy for you.

Over at Cal we never had any quarterbacks. The guys who played that position just had to know enough to hand the ball off to our Polish and Italian fullbacks. Then everybody would just run

48

over everybody. Stanford guys throwing their spirals and dodging tacklers never had a chance against our fullbacks and running guards.

★   ★   ★

Let me tell you, the differences were clear in those days. Stanford guys wore sports coats to the Big Game. Chances are, they'd be entertaining their mothers at luncheon before the game. We'd come down to Palo Alto in Levis and T-shirts, sloshed out of our minds. Then our fullbacks would bury their quarterbacks. You felt safe in a world like that.

I first got the message that things were changing about seven or eight years ago when some Stanford kid started talking to me about radical politics. Didn't he know, I asked, that Stanford guys are supposed to be members of the establishment, rich kids who end up working for their fathers' banks? It's terrible when a kid doesn't know what he's supposed to be.

★   ★   ★

Hell, we always had radicals over at Berkeley. Scruffy guys in Ike jackets who worked for the Daily Cal, didn't belong to fraternities and dated all those pale girls with acne. Guys who carried books around all the time.

We had radicals, and we were proud of them. Made us that much different from Stanford. A Stanford radical might be a guy who smoked cigars or bird-dogged his fraternity brother's girlfriend. He didn't give speeches at Sather Gate.

Now it's all different. Stanford even elected a bearded guy student body president. Worse yet, he married a folk singer and gets busted for draft evasion. That's what Cal guys are supposed to do. Then there's the rumpus over ROTC. Stanford guys are supposed to like the military. They're commissioned second lieutenants in the Air Force at birth.

★   ★   ★

The football team is the final straw. Stanford has no business beating any team from Arkansas.

What ever happened to Bob Anderson?

Disciples of Another Creed

*From its founding there was not a ghost of a chance
that Stanford would resemble other California
universities. Its students are a singular, changing lot,
and among their surprising attitudes is their view
of sport.*

One troubled night following the death of his son, Leland Stanford was visited in his sleeping chamber by the boy's ghost. Observing that the old railroad tycoon had been weeping over his tragic loss, the shade admonished him for such self-indulgence and made what seemed a capital suggestion:

"Father, do not spend your life in vain sorrow," it said to him. "Do something for humanity. Build a university for the education of poor young men."

So Stanford did.

That, at least, is one explanation for the founding of Leland Stanford Junior University on Leland Senior's stock farm in Palo Alto, Calif. And though the story may be apocryphal, Stanford people are rather fond of it, for it tends to bolster their conviction that, although their university was erected on solid ground, it was at least celestially inspired.

Californians have long held to the view that there is, indeed, something other-worldly about Stanford. It is a prestigious private school of unimpeachable academic and social standing in a state where public education, particularly at the university and college level, has made its highest marks. Stanford is hardly the poor boy's school that the ghost had in mind—tuition will rise to $2,850 in September—but it has been so generously favored with scholarships that nearly half its 11,500 students are receiving financial aid of some sort.

Athletically, Stanford confounds its rivals by competing in the collegiate major leagues with a male undergraduate student body of little more than 4,000, with relatively few purely athletic scholarships and with an approach to sport bordering on the cavalier. Two successive Rose Bowl victories over heavily favored Big Ten schools with a much more orthodox football orientation testify to the effectiveness of this studied nonchalance. Admittedly, it is no longer fashionable to attach cosmic significance to mere college football games. With the economic ax falling, college athletics departments, once the money trees, are rapidly becoming just additional flora in the groves of academe. But even with this changing attitude, Stanford's approach to big-time athletics seems outrageously casual.

"The schools we should be playing are Harvard, Yale and Princeton," says sociology professor Sanford Dornbusch, articulating a familiar Stanford complaint that invariably galls its colleagues in the Pacific-8 Conference. "But because of our physical isolation—airline costs, scheduling difficulties, etc.—we were to a large extent stuck in the Pacific-8. A lot of people wish we weren't. Athletes at Stanford are not heroes. Many of them feel they must counteract the image that they are animals. They feel a lot of pressure to do well academically and so they usually do. But the university really cares about them, about not exploiting them."

The Stanford athletic department is virtually self-supporting. The only direct funds it receives from the university are for partial support of the physical education program, an amount approximating $400,000 annually. The remainder of the department's $2.4-million budget comes from football gate receipts (Stanford owns its own 87,000-seat stadium), concessions and television revenue, its golf course, gate receipts from other sports, notably basketball, stadium and arena rentals, coaching camps and a gym store. With this income, the department has finished from $100,000 to $400,000 in the black for the past seven years. The $400,000 or so it spends on athletic scholarships is raised not by the university proper, but by the 4,000-member Stanford Buck Club, which is composed of alumni and "friends of the university," some of them transplanted Easterners who find in Stanford the same sort of private school *esprit* they had left behind.

A modern American university with a moneymaking athletic department can afford to assume a holier-than-thou posture before those less favored. Still, back-to-back Rose Bowl triumphs would seem an embarrassment to an institution that professes to have put football in its place as an extracurricular activity hardly more meaningful to the academic experience than folk dancing. And so it would, were it not for a certain psychological resourcefulness typical of Stanford. The wins over Ohio State and Michigan, Stanfordites will say, were of true significance because they represented triumphs of life-style. The seeds of these victories were sown not so much on the practice fields, it will be alleged, as in the psyches of the competitors. Stanford football players under their then coach, John Ralston, enjoyed extraordinary freedom. What they did off the field was their own concern. Discipline was not imposed from the outside; it was expected to come from within. The length of a player's hair, the cut of his clothes, were considered to be personal matters.

"You can't do in Palo Alto what you can do in Columbia, S.C.," said Ralston, who moves on to try his blend of freedom and inspiration on the professional Denver Broncos this year. "If I'd tried to dictate, say, hairstyles to these boys, I just wouldn't have had a football team."

While both Big Ten teams were secreted before the Rose Bowl game, Stanford players were roaming. And, while the Midwesterners adhered rigidly to their ball-control game plans, the Stanford teams literally winged it—first with Jim Plunkett, then with Don Bunce at quarterback.

"There was a great contrast in football philosophies," recalls Bunce, a serious young man. "Having so much more freedom gave us a sense of knowing why we were playing football. We were more imaginative. They were so predictable. Football is such a regimented game that sometimes you have to doubt how much of a part you play. I think when the Michigan and Ohio State teams read before the games about the 'Stanford swingers' it had to frustrate them a little, it had to give us an edge."

Although frantic instructions were being transmitted to him from the sidelines in this year's game, Bunce called his own plays in the last hectic Stanford drive that led to Rod Garcia's game-winning field goal against Michigan with only 12 seconds remaining to play. The field goal itself was a triumph of participatory democracy. When it became apparent that only Garcia, a 155-pound Chilean, could win the day for Stanford, Ralston advanced upon the little kicker prepared to deliver an appropriately inspirational message. The exact nature of his address was as yet unclear to him—Ralston has a disarming manner of unloading the most plonking homilies— but he felt the times called for something uplifting, like 'Kick it straight, kid." Ralston remembered with a shudder that Garcia's five missed field goals and one extra point had cost his team a shocker of a 13-12 loss to San Jose State in the regular season. As Ralston bore down on Garcia, he was intercepted by Defensive Tackle Greg Sampson.

"It would be better," said Sampson firmly, "if you didn't talk to him."

"I guess Greg thought I bugged Rod," said Ralston after Garcia, without benefit of coachly counsel, delivered the winning kick.

Defensive tackles do not talk that way to Woody Hayes, or even to Bo Schembechler.

The life-style contrasts in these Rose Bowl games were equally apparent in the performances of the bands on the field. Both the Ohio State and Michigan musicians marched militarily before the crowds in more or less traditional neo-John Philip Sousa getups. They played oldies but goodies expertly. The Stanford "Incomparables" appeared in red blazers, black flare pants, jaunty white fedoras and mod neckties. Their eight tubas were psychedelically adorned. Two of the bandsmen marched with bare feet painted white. Actually "march" is a misnomer; Stanford's musicians "walk rhythmically" and in step only when the mood is upon them. Their halftime shows, designed by an inner group called the "Stanford Marching Unit Thinkers"—SMUT—and their repertoire were exclusively contemporary. And not all of them played particularly well. One musician admitted that before the season he had not touched his instrument since he last performed with his junior high school orchestra.

Yet the Stanford bands, like the football teams, were popular successes. "These were victories," claimed band photographer Jon Erickson, "of West Coast culture over the ways of stodgy Middle America."

That Stanford should somehow be representing "West Coast culture" in an encounter of this sort is, in itself, a modern phenomenon. Not that Stanford hasn't usually set itself apart from the middle; it is just that its Ivy League yearnings seemed also to set it apart from the West. Since Stanford places no restrictions on out-of-state applicants and even encourages them, it is probably the least Californian of California colleges. About a quarter of its students come there from east of the Mississippi. In addition, Stanford lived a long time with a decidedly un-Western rich-kids image, one which it is now energetically and successfully shucking.

The "Stanford man" of years past was a happily familiar stereotype, particularly for traditionally antagonistic Cal men in nearby Berkeley. He would be a blond White Anglo-Saxon Protestant with a year-round suntan. He would drink Scotch, not beer, drive his own Buick convertible and play smashing tennis. He would wear a tweed coat, khaki trousers and white bucks. His evenings would be spent at "L'Ommie's"—L'Ommelette restaurant near the campus on El Camino Real. His girl friend—later, obviously, his wife—would perpetually be "in the East." He would be a young Republican.

The Stanford woman? Well, her name would be "Itsy" or "Bitsy" or some such plutocratic diminutive and she would be living testimony to the maxim that "nine out of 10 California women are beautiful; the 10th goes to Stanford."

Like all generalizations, these fell wide of the mark, but there was enough truth in them to sustain generations of Cal graduates. Now they are meaningless, since that particular Stanford is no more. The traditional athletic, political and sociological rivalry with Cal at Berkeley seems to have been reduced to a, well, academic question. By some magical process of democratization, the students at both of these great Bay Area universities seem completely interchangeable. If anything, the Stanford kids look more like the Berkeley kids than the Berkeley kids do.

"Stanford is much more radical than Berkeley," says Reeni Maharam, a Stanford senior and former song girl who is determinedly unradical. "A girl friend of mine had a sister who transferred out of here to Berkeley just to get straight."

And it does seem that Stanford's radical Establishment is more durable than those in comparable universities. Even before the recent resurgence of antiwar protests on campuses across the nation, Stanford had its share of demonstrations and confrontations—in January and February, for example, over the firing of H. Bruce Franklin, an English professor and Melville scholar whose fervent appeals on behalf of violent revolution led, finally, to a faculty hearing and Franklin's dismissal for, in carefully chosen words, "incitement to use of unlawful coercion and violence and increasing the danger of injury to others." At the press conference following the action—the first dismissal of a tenured professor following a faculty hearing in Stanford history—Franklin's wife stood at his side carrying an unloaded carbine. There followed demonstrations and incidents of vandalism and bomb threats, yet these were minuscule in comparison with the campus-wide antiwar disturbances of two years ago.

A longtime favorite radical objective has been the university's job-placement center, where military recruiters occasionally make unwelcome visitations and where so-called war-related industrial firms interview prospective job recruits. The Palo Alto area fairly crackles with electronic firms fulfilling government contracts, and Stanford's own considerable involvement in federally sponsored research is yet another source of discontent.

Doug McHenry, a black youth who led the ballot in the student election in 1971, sees something "basically insincere" about many of the demonstrations. "We blacks view the movement here with mixed emotions. Oh yes, once a year you will see a gathering of the concerned. Then the next you know, they're off skiing in Sun Valley. And by their senior year, they've cut their hair and are too busy trying to get into Harvard Law School to care."

In truth, Stanford is probably just what Professor Dornbusch calls it: "a terribly heterogeneous place. There is no typical Stanford kid anymore. There is, instead, an enormous variety of persons here, all of whom think they're in the minority."

Stanford has not come by this heterogeneity accidentally; it was sought. Admission to the university is determined by a complex and flexible formula involving academic standing, test scores, personal recommendations and achievement outside the classroom.

"Twenty years ago our students may all have come from the same middle-class background," says Dean of Undergraduate

Studies James Gibbs, exploring a familiar theme, "but our goal now is to get a mixture. If their academic standing is high enough we like to get concert pianists, artists and, yes, quarterbacks. We could, I suppose, admit everyone in the top 2% in high school, but this would not be a very interesting place if we did."

Where Stanford has made its most significant advances in enrollment is in the recruitment of minority students. Under the energetic leadership of President Richard W. Lyman, a 48-year-old Ivy League (Harvard graduate school) migrant, Stanford has, in Gibbs' words, "made a deliberate effort to meet its social responsibilities." Gibbs himself is black.

The results of this recruiting, which dates to a decision made following the assassination of Dr. Martin Luther King, have been startling. While the overall student population has increased by only 24 since 1968, Stanford has more than doubled its black enrollment—from 226 to 548. It has 368 Chicano students now, compared with 58 four years ago, and 61 American Indians, compared with 14. (The Indian students are not without influence, for upon their protest the university last month dropped the "Indians" nickname for its athletic teams on grounds it was racially debasing. Stanford thus became the first major sponsor of a sports team called Indians to do so. Stanford teams had been Indians since 1930, when the term replaced "Cardinals" or "The Cardinal," the official school color. The old name may now enjoy a comeback, although a "mascot search committee," shuffling through some 50 suggested names—including, of course, "Cowboys"—proposed in all sincerity that the teams adopt the sobriquet applied to last year's defensive line—"Thunderchickens." Thunderchickens?) A remarkably high number—85%—of Stanford undergraduates receive degrees. The rate among the minority students is even higher —88% get theirs.

On a somewhat subtler level, Stanford also has improved its relationships with another group protesting its oppression—women. It is no thanks to Mrs. Jane Lathrop Stanford that the school she and her husband endowed is today coeducational. She was opposed from the beginning to admitting members of her own sex into an institution of higher learning. It was only when Leland—no male chauvinist—argued that their son's school should serve "all the children of California" that she relented. But she surrendered only grudgingly, and in deference to her wishes Stanford's female applicants were to receive harsher scrutiny than the male. For many years, the male-female enrollment held at a ratio of nearly three to one. Understandably sensitive on this issue today, Stanford administrators point with some pride to an undergraduate enrollment that is now 4,094 men and 2,337 women. President Lyman hastens to emphasize that sexism is not an official policy of the school, that applicants are not judged on the basis of sex, that no formal quota exists and that "roughly the same proportion of women and men applicants are accepted." Furthermore, an informal survey shows the 10th California girl must be enrolled elsewhere now. Stanford has its proportion of pretty coeds.

The university has made enormous strides, academically as well as ethnically, in recent years. "Stanford," says Professor of Religion Dr. Robert McAfee Brown, an ardent civil libertarian, "is no longer a West Coast finishing school."

A 1969 survey by the American Council on Education would seem to substantiate these assertions. Stanford's faculty was ranked among the first five nationally in 16 fields of graduate study, a total exceeded only by Cal and Harvard. Stanford has six Nobel Laureates. Thirty of its departments out of 32 judged were rated "strong to distinguished" by the council—a figure equaled by Columbia and surpassed only by Cal, Harvard and Yale. Stanford's psychology and pharmacology departments were rated the best in the nation. Its engineering courses—chemical, civil, electrical and mechanical—were in the first four. All of its physical-science courses—chemistry, geology, mathematics and physics—were ranked in the top six. Stanford's business and law schools have long been considered first rate and its medical school has achieved international renown through the pioneer work in heart transplants undertaken by a team of surgeons under Dr. Norman Shumway and the synthesis of biologically active DNA by Dr. Arthur Kornberg.

Stanford's most ambitious gains, however, have been in the humanities, where it has been weakest. Of Stanford's seven presidents, only two have not been in the sciences or engineering—J.E. Wallace Sterling (1949-68) and Lyman, both historians. Sterling is credited with bringing about the university's overall academic renaissance and Lyman has been instrumental in improving the liberal-arts programs. Stanford is now rated fourth nationally in the classics, fifth in German and sixth in English by the Council on Education.

Such measurements are always deceptive and, as some educators have protested, they do not adequately represent the quality of undergraduate education. But Stanford is almost more graduate school than undergraduate. Of the 11,500 students enrolled, almost half are in graduate school, and there are nearly 150 more male graduate students than undergraduate. Stanford's growth as an increasingly important research center is underscored by the more than $50 million it receives annually in government grants.

"I see this school becoming more and more like a giant corporation," says undergraduate McHenry. "It is so concerned with research and development and government contracts, you wonder why it bothers having educators and administrators. What it needs is a good systems coordinator."

That Stanford is more corporation than university, says President Lyman, is "a widespread myth. I'm not saying the balance between teaching and research is ideal here or at any other research-oriented university. But you don't necessarily improve undergraduate education by cutting into research programs. You don't direct faculty that way. And you don't get grants unless students are involved."

Lyman, a slender, casually dressed man who might himself pass for a graduate student, is in a position familiar to all modern college administrators—the middle. On the one hand, he needs the research grants; on the other, he must preserve the university's intellectual independence.

"Some students think we're not fighting the battle," he says wearily. "But we are. I think it's remarkable that, considering the dependence we have on outside resources, we have remained independent."

Under Lyman, Stanford has taken positive measures to improve undergraduate programs. Stanford students, for example, have great latitude in selecting their major course of study. They may even create their own major if they can convince three faculty members and a sub-committee that what they have in mind is sound academically. They have the additional privilege of attending for two quarters one of the five Stanford overseas campuses—in France, Italy, Germany, Austria and England. There are also plans for a program that would allow undergraduates to study for a year in an African university. And Dean Gibbs, for one, sees nothing wrong with a student deciding to drop out for a time to work or simply to reassemble himself psychologically.

Whatever the reason, something must be working, for Stanford's undergraduates are hitting the books as never before. The J. Henry Meyer Undergraduate Library is doing a standing-room-only business during the week, and Sunday attendance has almost trebled over two years ago.

The resurgence of book learning would have gladdened the broken old heart of the founding father, although the university Leland Stanford envisioned is hardly the one that stands on his farm today. Stanford saw higher educaiton as preparation for "personal success and direct usefulness in life." A university should teach a person practical things, a trade. The old man's opinion, for example, that "the earth is inexhaustible in supplies for the gratification of every reasonable want of man" would hardly mesh with the birth-control views expressed today by Dr. Paul Ehrlich, the noted Stanford biology professor who sees the earth's supplies so nearly exhausted that he recently suggested the government reward women for not having babies.

But it was through hard, practical—some might say unscrupulous—work that Stanford earned his share of those inexhaustible supplies. Born on a farm in New York, he practiced law in Wisconsin, moved to California during the Gold Rush, made a small fortune as a successful merchant and a much bigger one as president of the Central Pacific Railroad, the West Coast's link with the first transcontinental line. He was Governor of California during the Civil War and a United States Senator at the time of his death in 1893.

Stanford was in many ways the ultimate 19th century *nouveau-riche* American capitalist—a bloated (260 pounds), glowering, bearded eminence. But he lavished great affection on his only child, Leland Jr., who was born when he was 44 and Jane 39. When young Leland expressed a mild and perhaps hereditary interest in trains, Stanford had a miniature railroad with 200 yards of track built for him on the farm. And when the adolescent Leland developed an interest in art collecting, Stanford saw to it that he could indulge his tastes in the culture capitals of Europe. He traveled extensively, and on one of these cultural explorations the boy fell desperately ill with typhoid fever. The illness lasted three weeks. Then, on March 13, 1884, the Stanfords wired home to San Francisco from Florence: OUR DARLING BOY WENT TO HEAVEN THIS MORNING AT HALF-PAST SEVEN. . . .

His grief was so great that Stanford's own life seemed endangered. In his delirium, he hallucinated. It was after a fitful evening in the company of visions that he advised Mrs. Stanford: "The children of California shall be our children." On Nov. 14, 1885 he donated three tracts of land, including the Palo Alto farm, to a board of trustees for the purpose of building a university in his son's name. The gift was conservatively estimated at $5 million. It was worth four times that amount by the turn of the century. In addition, he financed the college until his death, and insured that it received the bulk of his estate.

Few college campuses have been so favored economically and naturally, Stanford's first president, David Starr Jordan, described the farm in his autobiography:

"Bounding it on the Southwest, rises an irregular series of Coast Range ridges, known collectively as the Sierra de la Santa Cruz—'a misty camp of mountains pitched tumultuously.' Immediately behind the University estate, and forming its higher background, is the wooded Sierra Morena, 1,300 feet high, its cloak of redwood, oak and madrono diversified by thickets of chemisal. . . ."

The 8,800-acre campus is spacious, with long pathways through redwoods and eucalyptus groves. Little more than 30 miles south of San Francisco, but protected by sheltering mountain ranges to the east and west, Stanford is about 20 degrees warmer than the city during the summer. And if, as Stanford critics doggedly assert, there is a country-club ambience, so be it.

The Stanford family's fondness for Romanesque architecture is reflected in the rectilinear buff-colored stone buildings, covered arcades and half-circle arches. The university is affiliated with no church, but the total effect, particularly in the quadrangle area, is of a Spanish monastery. A swinging Spanish monastery.

Leland Stanford Junior University did not open for classes until Oct. 1, 1891, nearly six years after the founding. And as the then 67-year-old Stanford and his wife ascended to the stage for the dedication ceremonies, 400 students arose and shouted, "*Wah*-hoo! *Wah*-hoo! L!S!J!U! *Stan*ford!" It was a cheer they had improvised that very morning. Mercifully, it has been seldom heard since.

In the charter class was a young Iowan who would become the 31st President of the United States, and over the years Stanford was to have few more devoted alumni than Herbert Clark Hoover. He accepted the Republican Party's 1928 presidential nomination in Stanford Stadium. He founded the Food Research Institute on campus and was instrumental in organizing the Graduate School of Business. The 285-foot Hoover Tower houses the Hoover Institution on War, Revolution and Peace, and the Hoover home on campus is now the official residence of the university president.

Hoover was also Stanford's first undergraduate football manager and was, therefore, a key figure in the historic first "Big Game" with California in 1892. Some historians blame Hoover for an oversight—no football—which detracted only slightly from the dignity of the occasion. Still, when a facsimile ball—more of a punching bag, actually—was finally secured, Stanford won the game, 14-10. It was, of course, something of an upset.

Upsets, innovation and ingenuity have characterized Stanford's athletic history. Stanford's 1940 team, coached by Clark Shaughnessy, introduced the modern T formation to college football. Stanford's Ben Eastman revolutionized middle-distance running by breaking the world records for the quarter and half miles within two weeks. And by surpassing the quarter-mile record by a full second, from 47.4 to 46.4, he converted the event from a run to a dash. Stanford's Hank Luisetti changed basketball from a two-hand set-shot game to the modern version with his running, jumping one-hand push shot.

In Fullback Ernie Nevers, Stanford produced one of football's finest all-round athletes. But the school's football specialty over the past 30 years has been in the so-called "skill positions"—quarterback and receiver. Only Notre Dame has fielded as many outstanding quarterbacks, and Stanford's have been even more successful as professionals: witness Frankie Albert, John Brodie and Jim Plunkett. Three Stanford alumni—Brodie, Plunkett and Dave Lewis—are now playing quarterback in the National Football League. Stanford has also turned out such adept receivers as Bill McColl, Chris Burford, Gene Washington and Randy Vataha.

Curiously, the team most cherished at Stanford is one that scarcely threw the ball at all. But the "Vow Boys" of 1933-35 had a mystical quality that is the special Stanford mark. The Vow that separated them from the rest of the boys was taken when they were freshmen in 1932. It was a Monday practice following the varsity's fifth consecutive loss to USC. As the freshmen gathered in the center of the practice field, Quarterback Frank Alustiza summoned the team to gather around him.

"They'll never do that to us," Alustiza said. "We will never lose to USC."

"Let's make a vow on that!" shouted Halfback Bones Hamilton, caught up in the fervor the moment. They did, and USC never did beat them, losing 13-7, 16-0 and 3-0. It is beside the point that hardly anybody else ever beat the Vow Boys, either. In three years they won 25 games, lost four (two in the Rose Bowl) and tied two. Nineteen of their 25 wins were shutouts, including seven in a row in 1934.

But it is the Vow, not the record, that endears them to Stanford, where spirit, even among the seemingly disinterested undergraduates of today, is still a meaningful word. It is significant that Stanford football players regard their recent Rose Bowl victories not so much as triumphs of the flesh but of the spirit.

"In both games," said Bunce, "I didn't see how we could win. But we were ready. We were at a fairly high intellectual level."

Indeed, what is often mistaken for snobbery, intellectual or otherwise, is simply Stanford's penchant for setting itself apart. There is, as Professor Dornbusch suggests, an "isolation," whether real or just felt. This is what leads Stanford, athletically, to cast itself so often in the role of underdog.

"The reason you have to take your hat off to Stanford," says the school's sports historian, Don Liebendorfer (and how many schools have sports historians?), "is that we've done it the hard way. Here you have an expensive school with high admission requirements. The coaches have always made the best of what they've had and the kids have always put in that something extra. Something extra. That's the whole thing. That's the spirit of Stanford."

"Come join the band," the fight song resounds. "And give a cheer for Stanford red. . . ."

Somehow, some way, the entreaty seems almost irresistible.

The Voices of Spring

Robins are all well and good in their place, but they'll never replace Russ Hodges and That's Right for me.

I mean, who but a crazed ornithologist would regard the appearance of a red-breasted Turdus Migratorious as a harbinger of spring? To most of us, the resonant gargles of the resident broadcasters are synonymous with the vernal equinox.

It's always difficult to assess the significance of radio "sportscasters." Suffice to say that for at least several generations of Americans, they are as symbolic of the times as any other trivia. And, it is the trivia that preserves our identity.

Take the year 1938, a bad one overall. But to many of us, it will forever to be identified with marble fudge ice cream, Action Comics, the planet Krypton and Errol Flynn movies.

So it is with sports announcers, few of whom—fortunately—have any conception of their impact. But their voices—metallic, urgent—are part of the fabric of our lives.

★ ★ ★

I am certain that poor Harry Wismer was a monumental boor in the flesh, but his voice—"Blanchard approaches the ball"—is dear to me. Of course, as one grows older, those disembodied growls become, on occasion, more of an intrusion than an angelic visitation.

Besides, from these Olympian vistas, it's amusing to fire barbs at the earthling broadcasters. Sure Hodges frequently communicates to us through a mouthful of frankfurter and Simmons asks questions that require no response. That's right. But, by heaven, it's good to hear them again.

Basically, baseball broadcasters tend to be bigger personalities than their football counterparts, if one allows for a certain amount of duplication.

The baseball broadcaster is generally an anecdotist, a button-downed David Harum, who leisurely guides us through a warm

63

afternoon of mild exercise. The football man, on the contrary, is hyperthyroid, portentous, a doomsayer or evangelist. He is Billy Graham to baseball's Maharishi Mahesh Yogi.

Many of these artists are, of course, dual personalities, warring souls captured in the body of an aging child.

★   ★   ★

Take Simmons, the inevitable Lon. As a baseball announcer, this genial giant is a chummy sort who, for the most part, seems half-amused by the antics of his confreres on the diamond. One envisions him sitting there in full Giant uniform, propelling an occasional cud into a convenient cuspidor. He will probably shower with the rest of the gang after the last out is gloved.

The football Simmons is of a different breed. On these broadcasts, he speaks with the clipped diction of Walter Winchell or Bette Davis.

His emotions run away with him. He shouts. He sounds, for that matter, like all other football announcers.

And that's the difference, I think. Football broadcasting doesn't leave all that much room for individual expression. Every word the announcer utters seems of great moment. A computer could do the job as well.

★   ★   ★

Oh, I'll grant you, the game has produced its own creative geniuses—Ted Husing, Bill Stern, even Wismer. But I fear that, personal integrity aside, these pioneers were given to exaggeration and over-dramatization. These earlier radio men had an insurmountable advantage over us—they could say anything they wanted because we couldn't see what was happening. Television has changed all that.

But the baseball announcer comes to us intact through the ages, a wry and familiar philosopher, full of native wit.

Welcome back.

Lucky Devil, He Found Heaven

When he's not busy sportscasting, satanic Bill King gobbles peanut butter tortillas, studies Russian lit, watches ballet and barefoots it at sea with Hank the black cat

Like everything about him, Bill King's satanic countenance, with its beard, bristling mustache and almond-shaped eyes buried behind protruding cheekbones, is distinctive. But it is not the sort of kisser that inspires instant affection, particularly from television nabobs and superstitious old women.

A crone once chanced upon an unwitting King on the streets of Milwaukee. She identified him instantly as the Dread Adversary and began menacing him with her cane.

"I beg your pardon, madame," said King who, despite his diabolical mien, is unfailingly cordial to his elders. "I don't believe we"ve met."

"Oh, I know you," snarled the woman. "You, you . . . you are the devil himself." And she set about giving him his due.

"Aha," cried King, dodging the blows. "So you recognize me, do you?"

"Yes, I do, you devil you."

"Well, then," cooed King, twirling his mustache seductively, "we shall surely meet again. At my place down there."

The old woman emitted a strangled yelp, withdrew her cane and fled with remarkable haste.

King, of course, is not the Prince of Darkness. He is the play-by-play radio announcer for the National Football League's Oakland Raiders and the National Basketball Association's Golden State Warriors. But, as Ron Fell, long-time producer of King's football broadcasts, has observed, "Bill is not what you call your average run-of-the-mill sportscaster."

He certainly is not an ordinary announcer, or an ordinary anything else. King is a balletomane and opera buff, a serious student of Russion history, language and literature, a sailor of the high seas, a wine connoisseur and accomplished chef, a motorist who considers paying more than $200 for an automobile gross extravagance, and a trencherman who devours raw onions for breakfast.

The breadth of his interests, passions and eccentricities continually bewilders King's legion of friends, many of whom lead such entirely different lives that they have only King in common. To most of them, King appears to be several persons in one, and they are not far off the mark.

Announcing a sporting event, he can be so stimulated by the tumult that he flies into paroxysms of rage, anguish or joy. On most of these occasions King's strongest expletive is the mildly blasphemous "Holy Toledo," a phrase he has made a standard part of the Bay Area sporting vocabulary. But once he became so excited over a decision by an NBA official that he switched off his microphone, bounced the instrument off the press table and bellowed a locker-room obscenity at the offending referee as he passed within range.

Unfortunately for King, a crowd mike picked up the oath and broadcast it to a startled radio audience. Afterward he was rebuked by the usual assortment of church groups, outraged mothers, decency organizations and a precocious 10-year-old who wrote suggesting that if King could not exercise greater discretion on the air, he should seek "another avenue of employment." At the same time, he was heartily commended by a college fraternity for his forthrightness and sincerity.

It would be reasonable to expect that a live wire of this voltage would be bonkers at the conclusion of a broadcast. Indeed, King does require a moment or two to wind down after a game, or on hot days to dress up, since it is his practice to broadcast in his underwear when temperatures are excessive. But in no time at all he is blissfully journeying homeward in his latest jalopy, his nerves soothed by the thunderous harmonies of Wagner or Rimsky-Korsakov emanating from the car radio. The game is well behind him, lost perhaps in *Gotterdammerung*, and there is still time for a spot of Turgenev or Tolstoi before retiring.

King resides in Sausalito, the bohemian boating community across the Golden Gate Bridge from San Francisco. Twice divorced, he shares his passion for music and the sea, if not always for basketball and football, with his companion for the past 14 years, Nancy Stephens. They have never "bothered" to marry, although King's football broadcasting mate, Scotty Stirling, has said of their relationship, "It is as sound as any I've ever seen between a man and a woman."

It pleases King that his neighbors in Sausalito "don't know if a basketball is round or square." He assiduously avoids such San Francisco watering holes as Perry's or the Templebar, where chances of encountering someone versed in the nuances of the fast break or post pattern are far too promising. Sausalitans talk mainly about boats and sex, in roughly that order, and King would have it no other way. Since he abhors the limelight, he is not at all ruffled by the knowledge that citizens of his adopted community think of him as just another long-haired boat freak.

King apparently looks too hip for network television people, who are reluctant to put a man with long hair, a beard and a mustache on a national sports broadcast. What they fail to appreciate is that he is much more the product of his Midwestern upbringing than of his acquired West Coast bohemianism.

King was born 46 years ago on a farm outside Bloomington, Ill. At age seven, he and his recently widowed mother moved into town. Much of his childhood was spent huddled before the living room console listening to Cubs' Broadcaster Bob Elson. King and Elson's disembodied voice spent so much time together that the boy began to sound like the man. Years later, when King was auditioning for an announcing job with the San Francisco Giants, the late Russ Hodges, then the Giants' lead broadcaster, quickly identified him as a Cub fan. "With people my age, you can tell where they're from by the baseball announcer they sound like," says King.

Though short and slight, King played catcher on his high school baseball team—television star McLean Stevenson was one of his pitchers—and for one giddy moment contemplated a professional career. Instead, he was drafted into the Army after graduation in 1945 and dispatched to Guam. There he fell in love with the blue Pacific, vowing someday to return to her aboard a great sailing vessel. He also was an Armed Forces Radio disc jockey, an occupation the garrulous King found particularly appealing because it afforded him unlimited opportunity to talk without interruption. The air and the sea. Prophetically, they would become his vocation and avocation.

After the service, King eschewed college and worked as a broadcaster in the Illinois towns of Pekin, Quincy and Peoria. In Peoria he was one of three announcers doing the Bradley University basketball games. Chick Hearn, now the voice of the Lakers and with King one of the two or three best pro basketball announcers, was one of the others. King moved on to Lincoln, Neb. before he packed up his sailing manuals on Memorial Day 1958 and set off for San Francisco, where he had no prospect of a job but could be near his beloved Pacific.

He was a man of leisure for only a short time, thanks to his friendship with Hodges, another Giant broadcaster, Lon Simmons and Bud Foster, a veteran Bay Area sportscaster. In 1958 King worked with Foster on University of California football and basketball, then in 1959 he joined Hodges and Simmons as the third man on the Giants' broadcasting team. Three years later, he signed on with the Warriors, newly transplanted from Philadelphia. In a moment of whimsy, he also grew a beard. Warrior Owner Franklin Mieuli, who is as hirsute as a bear today, was then a clean-shaven broadcasting executive. Despite his legendary eccentricity, he shared at least some of the conservative views of his industry. Remember, this was 1962, a time when even college students were beardless youths and only jazz musicians and atomic physicists sprouted whiskers. Image was a big word then. But Mieuli took a courageous stand with King. "I am not going to tell a man what he must do with his face," he boldly announced. The beard stayed, although before it had become an issue King had intended to shave it off.

In 1966 he joined the Raiders. Because he was only the radio announcer, King's photograph did not appear in the team's press book, an omission that troubled him not at all. Unlike so many broadcasting popinjays, he is not a vain man. His face does not so much delight as amuse him.

King discovered culture in 1965. "Nancy took me to a ballet, and though I couldn't explain why, I was hooked," he says. "I just plunged right into it. The opera came next. I'd listen to the music while working on the boat, but I couldn't imagine going to a performance. Now we haven't missed an opera in San Francisco in six years."

King approaches each of his myriad pastimes with a scholar's meticulousness. His brain is omnivorous, ravenously chomping on each passing intellectual morsel. Before he became an opera regular, King studied the lives of the composers. He has taught himself to read Russian and has a vocabulary of about 1,000 words. Although he is only a student in the adult school of the College of Marin, he recently was invited to fill in for an absent professor in a course on the Russian literature of protest.

On a typical stopover with the Warriors in New York this winter, King turned his back on the swinging East Side taverns favored by many of his traveling companions and trotted off to Lincoln Center to hear an Andre Watts piano recital and the Metropolitan Opera's production of *Boris Godunov*. He dined exclusively in ethnic restaurants and endlessly prowled the museums.

King has been unwittingly called a gourmet. It is a word he detests, one he ranks alongside "intellectual" as among the most abused in the language. He prefers to think of himself as a gastronome whose tastes observe no bounds. King may dine on Veal Orlov in the plushest San Francisco or New York restaurants, or he may gobble nauseous combinations of foods—peanut butter and popcorn is one favorite—to the discomfort of his confreres in the broadcasting booth. "You can't believe some of the things he eats," says Stirling, turning green at the thought. "God Almighty, peanut butter tortillas!"

King may be at his happiest preparing massive Russian meals in his own kitchen. "I put the Don Cossack chorus on the hi-fi for mood music," he says, "and we all sit about drinking Stolichnaya vodka and eating zakushi, piroshki, borscht and shashlik. The whole thing takes about five hours. By about three in the morning we're all sitting there crying in our Stolichnaya, happy as can be."

King is the soul of affability away from the microphone, but Warrior road trips have become almost void of stimulating conversation for him. When Tom Meschery, who shared King's interests in poetry and Russian literature, played for the team some years ago, seminars into the early morning were the rule. Now King finds that he loses his audience when the talk turns away from such subjects as Rick Barry's floor play or the rebounding of Clifford Ray. A recent disquisition by King in a Los Angeles coffee shop on Pasternak's reliance on coincidence in his *oeruvre* did not set other tongues wagging. King merely shrugs his shoulders on these lamentable occasions and presses on to something of broader interest, like the literary integrity of Solzhenitsyn.

It is understandable, then, that King abruptly departs the sports world as soon as the basketball season ends and sets sail aboard his 44-foot ketch *Varuna* for ports far removed from the cries of "DEE-fense." He is not seen again until football begins.

His trips have taken him as far asea as the Georgia Strait and Hawaii. But King's sharpest memory is of a journey that he, Nancy, their seagoing black cat Hank and several friends made a few summers ago to explore the islands and inlets of British Columbia. There King achieved a kind of Nirvana.

"We had sailed into the Princess Louisa Inlet," he says. "I awoke on the boat early one morning and could hear nothing but the rush of water. I climbed up on deck and for as far as I could see there were waterfalls. I counted 39 of them. I just sat there listening. I don't think I've ever felt such a sense of peace. When we left, I kept asking myself, 'Why? Why are we leaving?'"

Varuna is a handsome vessel of Honduras mahogany, teak and white oak. King has nothing but contempt for fiberglass boats, craft he denigrates as "plastic throwaways." With its good wood, *Varuna* is more precious to him than even his Russian grammar or breakfast onions, and he lavishes constant attention on her. The boat's shimmering beauty is in marked contrast to the dilapidated appearance of King's automobile of the moment. He does not accept the popular notion that a car should be washed and serviced from time to time. His life is a mess of contradictions, but never more so than when he and Nancy, both dressed to the nines, pull up in front of the stately San Francisco opera house in a vehicle that could have transported the Joad family West.

King simply drives his cars until they ignite, explode or quietly succumb to the infirmities of advanced years. He was obliged to flee a 1956 Buick several years ago when it burst into flames with 128,000 on the odometer. He had been driving a 1954 Ford for more than a year when a missing tooth in the flywheel led to a dreadful commotion under the hood. The transmission fell out of his 1961 Oldsmobile after 120,000 miles. Stirling feels he may have shamed King into abandoning a 1960 Pontiac last fall when he advised him that without floorboards on the passenger side, riding with him was something of a hazard. King, who apparently had been oblivious to this defect, glanced down in alarm and reluctantly conceded that Stirling might have a point. When he turned the car over to the junkyard it had gone a courageous 135,000 miles.

King could probably double his annual income of roughly $50,000 if he made himself available in the summer for commercials and promotional work, but the prospect of performing such lucrative tasks appalls him. His ultimate goal is to abandon broadcasting altogether and cruise the seas, an objective he was approaching a year ago when a series of misguided investments forced postponement of the odyssey. In an industry bursting with giant egos, King, with his lack of pretension and wanderlust, is an anomaly.

"You run into a lot of schlocks in this business, guys who are in it for the glory of rubbing elbows with the stars and of being called stars themselves," says Producer Fell. "Bill is just not that kind. I've never met anyone in any walk of life with more depth in more areas. And he is a totally principled individual."

"Bill's honesty may be at the root of many of his frustrations as a broadcaster," says Hank Greenwald, a former King partner on Warrior broadcasts. "When you're doing a basketball game and you say a guy has dribbled out of bounds and the official doesn't see it, you are left there with nothing to substantiate what you've just said. Bill just flat out says the official goofed."

King achieved a kind of apoplectic grandeur assessing the officials' performance in a Warrior loss to the Knicks in New York this season. "Under the pressure of a Garden crowd, the officials choked here tonight," he advised his listeners. "I tried to keep my mouth under control, but the officials were so abominable I couldn't help myself."

"King may be the greatest basketball announcer in the world," says one of his confirmed fans, "but I just wish he'd give up trying to officiate every game." King's riposte to such thrusts is to say that the officials greatly influence basketball games, that the announcer is closer to the action than in most other sports and can see what is happening, and that a man must say what is on his mind.

King's penchant for saying what is on his mind has caused Mieuli financial embarassment. Several seasons ago the Warriors' owner was fined $500 by NBA Commissioner Walter Kennedy for critical comments King and Greenwald had made on the air about the officiating. Mieuli paid grudgingly, offering obeisance to a creature he had championed, a strong commissioner. But he grumbled afterward that the next time his announcers were challenged, the strong commissioner could "stuff it."

Although King's basketball broadcasting salary is paid by the Warriors, he is as much a houseman as John Dean. (The Raiders have final approval on their announcers, but King is technically an employee of KNBR during the football season.) In the course of one week this season, King accused the Warriors of being "static" and "lethargic," questioned Coach Al Attles' strategy of benching rookie Keith Wilkes when he appeared to be enjoying a hot night, described Barry's play as being without snap, twitted the Warriors for failing to make use of a mismatch under the basket, described a bad Warrior quarter as "the worst this season," and decided that one contest was so shabbily played "it had only a few moments approaching artistry." In a game with Phoenix, King even defended an official's decision that went against the Warriors. "The fans are pretty irate over that charging call, but I thought it was a pretty good one myself," he said.

Along with candor, there is stagecraft in a King broadcast. When he seems most frenetic, he is still in command, capable even of correcting his usually flawless grammar. "It could have been him. No, it could have been he. What's wrong with me, anyway?" King builds tension with his voice, carefully avoiding the error of peaking too soon. In the final minutes of the Raiders' melodramatic 28-26 playoff victory over Miami last December, he artfully created an image of the Miami end zone as "The Promised Land." When the Raiders finally reached Canaan with 26 seconds left on the scoreboard clock, it was as if Moses himself had negotiated the yardage.

"The Promised Land is eight yards away . . . Stabler is looking, looking, looking . . . he's rolling out, he's hit, he floats the ball up there . . . it's a touchdown. A touchdown. A touchdown. I can't even see the receiver. Clarence Davis. It looks like Clarence Davis. He's being mobbed . . . Stabler was hit as he threw . . . he was falling down. . . ."

That King recognized Davis as the survivor in that Sargasso Sea of players, officials and spectators was "incredible" in Stirling's opinion.

How has this paragon of the airwaves remained so obscure? Principally, by preference. King is a radio, not a television, man, and radio men today are as aviators to astronauts. He is a prisoner of his time, the Great Depression, when radio was all there was.

"I feel a strong obligation to radio and the radio listener," he said one recent afternoon, hunched over a cup of tea in his charming hillside house. He was barefoot, which he usually is when not at the opera house or the ball park. His feet are like slabs, his soles the consistency of concrete from clomping on boat decks. "I envision a shadowy image out there sitting next to the radio. I'm his eyes. If I can choose the right words to move and excite him, to tie his stomach in a knot, I've done my job and there is a beautiful satisfaction.

"Television doesn't provide this challenge. In TV you're the tool of some director who can interrupt your verbal flow to point out some girl the camera has stumbled across in the stands, and whom you must therefore talk about. You're a puppet. I've been a gadfly for so many years that I don't think the network people could tolerate me. And I doubt if I could tolerate them. Our schedules just don't match.

"Besides, look at this puss. I look mean on television, so I have to smile all the time. It's ridiculous. I know one TV guy who got fired because some station manager decided his lips were too moist. What would they do with a bearded guy who looks like the devil?

"I've often thought maybe my life has been a waste, that I might have been a Russian scholar by now at some university. But if I were, I might be thinking my life was a waste because I had never been out into the real world. I suppose I will always be asking myself what I'm going to do when I grow up. But I'm living on my own terms. I like what I do, and I've got time to do all these other things that have nothing to do with what I do. And when I leave my home and drive over the Golden Gate Bridge and see the changing panorama of light hitting beautiful hilly San Francisco, I say to myself, 'What other sports announcer in the world can drive to work and have all this?"

His pal Stirling says it even better: "Bill King has beaten the system."

The World's Greatest Runner

Not long ago, Sports Illustrated *magazine, surely the most literate publication in a field dominated by movie-magazine mentality, published a compilation of statistics which seemed to prove that O.J. Simpson was the best college running back in history.*

Simpson's physical dimensions, his track times and his accumulated yardage figures were measured alongside those of such certified immortals as Red Grange, Tommy Harmon and Glenn Davis. Simpson, this data seemed to establish, was bigger, faster and more productive than any of the earlier heroes.

Well, I'm not one to argue with such impressive statistical evidence, although most experts would agree, I think, that it's folly to make comparisons between athletes who competed in different eras. It's also irrelevant.

There's no question a man of Simpson's size and speed would have been a terror playing against the Lilliputians of Grange's period.

★ ★ ★

But it's all relative. And the important thing in college football is not so much cold statistics as memory.

I like to consider myself a running back aficionado. To me, they are the soul of the game, both on the college and the professional levels. I have only a passive interest in passers. They are the game's supervisory personnel; the runner is the romantic figure, the gallant loner escaping the bad guys.

I collect my runs with the zeal of a philatelist. And I'd have to say my favorite was one I never saw

It occurred, quite naturally, in the first year for me of dedicated fanhood. Until 1941, my interest in football—which then meant University of California football—had been at best sporadic. As a tot I'd been vaguely aware of the great Thunder Teams and of the achievements of Bottari and Chapman. Still, I was much more interested then in Errol Flynn movies and "sword fighting."

★   ★   ★

But in the fall of 1941, I sat for free in the tumultuous traffic boy section in Berkeley's Memorial Stadium. And I was truly smitten. For one, I fancied myself to be a broken field runner of considerable attainment, a fiction cruelly exploded only a few years later.

Kid fans, of course, are unabashed hero-worshippers. And we all had our own. Mine was a runtish halfback of modest talent named Al Derian. I liked Derian because he was an elusive runner and because, at about 160 pounds, he seemed so much smaller than the brutes around him.

Derian's every move on the field drew shrill cheers from this loyal admirer. If he should so much as gain 10 yards I proclaimed him another Grange.

In point of fact, Derian did have a good season in 1941. He was his team's leading scorer with six touchdowns—an achievement made meaningful only when one considers how rarely the Golden Bears of that vintage scored.

★   ★   ★

It was my fondest desire to see Derian play a Stanford team led by Frankie Albert in what then genuinely seemed to me to be the Big Game. But only a day before the game I collapsed with an embarrassing and, for me, heart-breaking attack of the mumps.

Fortunately, my illness was rewarded with a small bedside radio. And, as I lay there in an agony of disappointment, I switched on the Big Game. Stanford kicked off, and on the first play from scrimmage, California lined up single wing right.

"Derian's got the ball . . . he's at the 45, the 35, the 20 . . . he scores for California."

It was only a 46-yard run, but it won the game for my team and it was made by my hero. I wept with joy.

O.J. Simpson will never do that for me.

He Changed a Game Singlehandedly

Hank Luisetti shot the ball with one hand while he hung in midair. The Establishment smirked, but the sport has not been the same since.

The tall man with the gray streaked hair knelt alongside the small blond boy. He hefted the child-sized basketball in his large hands and, with a casual underhand flip, tossed it into the wastebasket across the room.

"No fair using two hands," said the boy. "You're supposed to shoot one-handed, the way you always did."

The man retrieved the ball, reassumed a kneeling position and, with his left hand under the ball and his right poised at eye level, flipped it into the basket again.

"Grandpa," the boy asked, "were you the greatest basketball player ever?"

"Some people say I was, Michael," Hank Luisetti answered.

"Well, you're not as good as Rick Barry."

"Maybe not," said Luisetti, flashing his U-shaped grin. "But what you don't know, Michael, what you can't know, is that the times are different. Very, very different."

*   *   *

Dr. Bill Northway, the Stanford basketball team's physician, was taping Hank Luisetti's ankles in the locker room at Madison Square Garden. Outside, it was windy and damp but warm for December. Inside the arena a crowd of 17,623, the largest of the year, was noisily lamenting Georgetown's 46-40 defeat of New York University in the first game of a big holiday doubleheader. But Georgetown-NYU was a mere preliminary to the event the crowd had really come to see, the match between Clair Bee's Long Island University Blackbirds, winners of 43 consecutive games, and the Stanford Indians, defending Pacific Coast Conference champions and 45-38 upset winners two days before over Temple, the second-best team in the East.

What the fans most wanted to see on Dec. 30, 1936 was Stanford's right forward, Luisetti, who had been setting scoring records by shooting the ball, in defiance of prevailing basketball dogma, with one hand.

After only a year of varsity play, Luisetti was a legend on the Pacific Coast. He had scored 32 points in 32 minutes in the opening game of the conference championship series the previous March against Washington. In another game Stanford had trailed Southern Cal by 15 points with 11 minutes left in a contest to determine the conference's Southern Division leader. Then Luisetti broke loose, scoring 24 of his 30 points, and Stanford won 51-47.

Teams rarely scored more than 45 points in a game then, and 20 points was considered extraordinary for an individual. It was an era when the clock was rarely stopped, when free throws were awarded sparingly and when a center jump following every basket was required in most sections of the country. A player who seemed able to score at will was the stuff of legend.

Still, the East had to be shown. Pacific Coast basketball was regarded in New York with mild contempt. On a similar holiday tour the year before, a University of California team was trounced 41-26 by NYU. That Cal team went on to split four games with Stanford during the conference season. Long Island University of Brooklyn, led by 6'8" Center Art Hillhouse and two-handed set shot artists Julie Bender and Ben Kramer, was the class of the East in the 1936-37 season, and the East was the class of the nation.

The Eastern teams played ball-control offense and man-to-man defense. They shot the ball in the traditional manner, and they rarely shot at all until the ball had been worked in with half a dozen passes or more.

Stanford's team was an enigma to Easterners. In their workouts Luisetti and his teammates seemed to be approaching the epochal conflict between Eastern orthodoxy and Western inconoclasm with an attitude bordering on the frivolous. At the West Philadelphia railroad station after the Temple win, they were observed rolling oranges into a cocked hat. They joked with New York reporters, laughing off suggestions that they would soon be sobered by their meeting with the Blackbirds. Their resolute amiability earned them the sobriquet "Laughing Boys." And those who watched them shooting one-handed during practice were moved to laughter—or derision. "I'll quit coaching if I have to teach one-handed shots to win," snapped Nat Holman, the City College of New York coach and the ranking savant of Eastern basketball. "They will have to show me plenty to convince me that a shot predicated on a prayer is smart basketball. There's only one way to shoot, the way we do it in the East—with two hands."

Stanford Coach John Bunn squirmed at intimations that he was some kind of radical. As a player at Kansas under Phog Allen and a former student of basketball's inventor, Dr. James Naismith, he protested that his credentials as a traditionalist were in order. But one look at young Luisetti swishing one-handers from 20 feet away had convinced him there was room for innovation.

Bunn was God-fearing, high-minded and sobersided, but he also believed athletics should be fun, so he gave his spirited charges the freedom to develop their individual skills. On offense, the Stanford players roamed like prarie dogs, switching positions to meet changing situations. Luisetti, the most liberated free-lancer of them all, might play the post, bring the ball downcourt or switch from the left to the right side at will. On defense the Indians played a combination zone and man-to-man that Bunn called a "team defense." Here again, switching positions was perfectly acceptable. To Eastern audiences, it all smacked of anarchy.

It was hardly that. For all of their free-wheeling, the Stanford players were highly disciplined and specialized. Left Forward Howell (Handsome Howie) Turner was Luisetti's height (6'2½") and a fine all-round player. The guards were 6'1" Bryan (Dinty) Moore, an inspirational player and a defensive demon, and 6'4" Jack Calderwood, an exceptional rebounder who was nicknamed "Frankenstein" or "Spook" because of his lumbering gait and ominous mien. Art Stoefen, at 6'4½" the tallest man in the lineup, was the center.

Principally because of its East-West flavor, the LIU-Stanford game received surpisingly good advance publicity during a typically busy news week in the newspaper-rich New York of the 1930s. The Spanish Civil War was Page One material, as were the travails of the recently abdicated King Edward VIII. Business, as usual, was ready for a big comeback, and President Roosevelt was urging Congress to restore NRA reforms. *You Can't Take It with You* and Clare Boothe's *The Women* had just opened on Broadway, as had motion pictures starring Shirley Temple and the newest challenger to her supremacy as the cutest little thing around, Bobby Breen. The *Daily News'* crackerjack headline writers were in top form: BOY STOLEN BY MADMAN, AX MURDER IS CLIMAX OF YULE REVELRY, DAD DIES AS GIRL LOSES SPELLING BEE, NEEDY MOTHER ABANDONS BABY AT WRONG POORHOUSE.

As Dr. Northway finished the taping, Luisetti good-naturedly ruffled the doctor's hair and pulled the necktie from beneath his vest for good luck. Then he and his teammates trotted into the magical arena. The Stanford players were hardly bumpkins. Luisetti and Calderwood were from San Francisco, Turner was from the Bay Area community of Piedmont, and Moore and Stoefen were from Los Angeles. But the sight of the packed Garden flabbergasted them.

"The first thing I saw was a giant neon sign," recalls Stoefen. "Then I looked up and saw what seemed to be thousands of fireflies. They were cigarettes glowing in the darkness. And through the haze of smoke, I finally saw people, people as far and as high as I could see."

"We were terribly tense all of a sudden," says Turner. "I don't think any of us had been to New York before. Most of us had never been out of California. We needed something to loosen us up. Mostly, we needed what we always seemed to get—something incredible from Hank."

The Blackbirds controlled the opening tap, and after a series of deft passes worked the ball under the basket to Hillhouse, who scored easily. On Stanford's first possession Turner was fed a pass in the right corner. The ball was slightly behind him and he started to tumble out of bounds as he reached for it. Instinctively, he threw the ball toward the basket anyway. He quickly scrambled to his feet to assume his position on defense when he noticed that a center jump had been called.

"Did that thing go in?" he asked Moore. Moore said it had, and the entire Stanford team burst into laughter. The Laughing Boys were now in the proper frame of mind to play their game.

The score was 11-11 midway in the first half, but already it was apparent that LIU was bewildered by the "team defense," the fast-break offense and Luisetti, who seemed to be everywhere, stealing the ball, rebounding over Hillhouse, passing with accuracy and lofting his one-handers from every angle.

"The first one came after a fake and a pivot near the foul line," Luisetti recalls. "It was over their big man. He looked at me and said, 'You lucky so-and-so.' He didn't say a word when the next one dropped in."

The crowd, which had pulled hard for Long Island University's team early in the game, was suddenly entranced by the black-haired dervish and his carefree companions. When the Indians left the court with a 22-14 halftime lead, the fans awarded them a standing ovation.

The second half was no contest. LIU went a full seven minutes without scoring, and Luisetti was in complete control of the tempo. He shot only when it was an inescapable obligation, preferring to dazzle the spectators with the baffling variety of his passes. Still, he led all scorers with 15 points as Stanford eased to a 45-31 victory. Later he would be named the outstanding athlete to perform in the Garden that year. The cheering New York fans, helpless Indian captives, sensed they had just witnessed a revolution.

Indeed, they had, as the press acknowledged the following day. "Overnight, and with a suddenness as startling as Stanford's unorthodox tactics, it had become apparent today that New York's fundamental concept of basketball will have to be radically changed if the metropolitan district is to remain among the progressive centers of court culture in this country," Stanley Frank pontificated in the *Post*. "Every one of the amiable clean-cut Coast kids fired away with leaping one-handed shots which were impossible to stop."

Said *The New York Times:* "It seemed Luisetti could do nothing wrong. Some of his shots would have been deemed foolhardy if attempted by anybody else, but with Luisetti shooting, these were accepted by the enchanted crowd."

The Stanford-LIU game was no mere intersectional upset. It was a pivotal game in the sport's history, introducing the nation to modern basketball. Players throughout the country began shooting on the run and with one hand. The deliberate style of play would give way to the fast break, the man-to-man would yield to the zone and combination defenses, and the following season the center jump after goals would be abandoned forever. Scoring suddenly increased, and a game that had served, in many areas, merely to fill the gap between the baseball and football seasons abruptly began to enjoy widespread popularity of its own. For anything big to happen then, it had to happen in New York. Luisetti and the Laughing Boys happened there in the winter of 1936.

Despite its color and dash, Stanford may not have been the first modern basketball team, but there is no disputing that Luisetti was the first modern basketball player. What astonished Garden fans was not so much that he shot, rebounded, dribbled, passed and played defense better than anyone on the court, but that he performed almost all these things in unorthodox ways. He dribbled and passed behind his back, and he appeared to shoot without glancing at the basket. When he drove, he soared like a hawk, looking left and right before he released a mid-air shot.

"Hank could stay up so long he was like a ballet dancer," Turner says. "He could fake while driving at a time when people just drove, period. Forty years ago he was making moves that still are considered exceptional today."

"It would be unfair to compare anyone who played then with the modern players," says Howie Dallmar, a former coach and player at Stanford. "But no one now—I mean no one—is as far ahead of his contemporaries as Hank was of his. He was at least 20 years ahead of his time. The guy revolutionized the game."

Luisetti is now 59 years old and his face has filled out, resulting in a startling resemblance to Jack Dempsey. He remains physically fit, although the only exercise he gets is walking. He has been a widower for the past three years, and between business trips he lives with either his 81-year-old mother in San Francisco or in the nearby homes of his son and daughter. His grandson Michael is a frequent companion.

Although unfailingly friendly, Luisetti is a private man. "Very few people ever got close to Hank," old teammate Calderwood says. "I hesitate to call him shy, but there is a reserve about him, a reserve that never showed on the basketball floor."

Luisetti has only recently begun going to basketball games again. He almost never watches Stanford but he has grown fond of the Golden State Warriors now that they are playing with championship verve.

"They can really shoot," says Luisetti. "It's a shooter's game today. When I was holding clinics, all I could interest the kids in was shooting. But look what's happened. If a team once shot 35% it was hot; now 50% seems average. And they're so big. At my height, I'd have to be a backcourt man today. I'd play about the way Jerry West did, moving the ball around, setting people up. That man played the game the way it should be played. Of course, it's harder to drive now—and I did a lot of that. The big men clutter up the area under the basket. It's worth your life to go in there. I think they're going to have to widen the court or raise the basket."

When he attends Warrior games Luisetti often dresses in a red and black warmup jacket and gray slacks, quite a departure from the crisp suits he usually wears as president of the E. F. MacDonald travel company's West Coast region. Sitting among the fans in the arena he is neither business executive nor old hero. No one in the place seems to have the slightest idea who he is.

✦　✦　✦

Angelo (Hank) Luisetti was born in San Francisco. His family lived on the northern slope of Russian Hill, a neighborhood of narrow wooden and stucco houses. From the top of the hill, the Bay can be seen blue-gray below, and in the distance are the orange towers of the Golden Gate Bridge. It is the quintessential San Francisco neighborhood, heavily Chinese now, but in Luisetti's time mostly Irish and Italian. His parents were of no-nonsense, old-country stock, their children aggressively New World. Sports became part of their generation gap.

Luisetti's father immigrated to San Francisco from northern Italy a few months after the great earthquake of 1906. It was not a bad time to arrive because of the opportunities awaiting those willing to rebuild a fallen city. Steven Luisetti learned to cook. He became a popular chef and he eventually bought his own restaurants, Louis' Fashion and the Sutter Grill.

The Luisetti's had one child, a skinny boy with legs so bowed that he was obliged to wear painful braces to straighten them. The family home was only three blocks from the Spring Valley (now Helen Wills) playground, a tiny, lopsided asphalt pile next door to a bowling alley. The playing area was so limited that the tennis court bisected the basketball court, and the two games could not be played simultaneously. Nevertheless, Helen Jacobs learned to play tennis there and Hank Luisetti learned to play basketball.

On foggy mornings the playground director, a tall young woman in a blue middy blouse and gray skirt named Rose McGreevy (now Mrs. Clifton Fogarty) would open the gates to find a solitary youngster splashing through the puddles on the misshapen court, flinging a basketball one-handed at the hoop as if he were hurling a discus. It was the only way he could reach the basket.

"We called him Angelo then," says Mrs. Fogarty, now 75. "I can never call him anything but that. The Hank business came later. He was always there an hour before I got to the playground. He likes to say I taught him everything he knows. What a laugh! He was such a natural. There wasn't anything I could teach him except to be a good boy, which he already was."

"I still remember those days," says Ed Dougery, a reporter for the *San Francisco Chronicle* who was a playmate of Luisetti's. "We wore dirty cords, tennis shoes and ragged sweaters. Sometimes we wore caps, the flannel kind you see in old movies. Our playground was too small for baseball, but sometimes we'd play the kids from North Beach in softball. We'd lose the game, then they'd beat the hell out of us. But not Angelo. He was a gentleman. And so was the big kid from the Beach who always wore a dark blue sweater, cords and his brother's San Francisco Seals cap. Joe DiMaggio. Baseball was his game. Basketball was Angelo's."

Luisetti was not so much a scorer at Galileo High as a master playmaker and defensive specialist, qualities that were much more admired in the days when championships were won by scores of 14-12. But as a freshman at Stanford in the 1934-35 season, he averaged better than 20 points a game. In his first varsity appearance he tried nine shots from the floor against College of the Pacific and sank them all. He set new scoring records each year he was on the varsity and as a senior he totaled 50 points in a game against Duquesne. His Pacific Coast Conference single-season record of 232 points survived for 12 years before being broken by Bill Sharman of USC and George Yardley of Stanford.

On March 5, 1938 he broke the national collegiate four-year scoring record in melodramatic fashion against California. With the historic point—No. 1,533—safely recorded, Luisetti leaped for a loose ball and collided with boyhood chum Dougery, who played forward for Cal. His head thumped against the floor and, as Harry Borba wrote in the San Francisco Examiner, "He was out as completely as Haile Selassie from Addis Ababa." He lay there unconscious as teammates and opponents formed a death watch around him.

Dougery stood off to one side, feeling "like the man who shot Lincoln. People kept asking me if I did it on purpose. 'Hell,' I kept saying, 'we went to grade school together.'"

Luisetti was helped from the floor as the partisan Cal crowd sat in silence. Had he broken the scoring record and ended his career on the same night? No. Minutes later he reappeared. The first time he touched the ball he scored. He finished the evening with 22 points, and he and Dougery double-dated afterward, dancing with their girls at the Mark Hopkins Hotel to the foot-tapping sounds of Orrin Tucker.

It was not the first time that season Luisetti had been resurrected. On Jan. 23, he collided with USC's Dale Goodrich, father of the Lakers' guard, and fell to the floor bleeding from a cut above the eye. He was stitched up in the locker room, returned to the court and scored immediately from 30 feet out.

Stanford defeated Oregon 59-51 for its third consecutive Pacific Coast Conference championship in Luisetti's last collegiate game. He scored 26 points in a virtuoso performance that brought the Stanford Pavilion crowd to its feet long before he left the game. Roy Cummings of the San Francisco Call-Bulletin was so moved by the experience that he rhapsodized, "When the future fans start talking about the basketball stars of their days, those who witnessed Hank Luisetti and the Stanford teams of 1936-37-38 will shake their heads and say, 'My lad, you never saw Luisetti.'"

No one saw Luisetti on a basketball court the next season. A wretched patchwork movie, Campus Confessions, earned him $10,000 from Paramount Pictures and, presumably because basketball was played in the film, a year's suspension from the Amateur Athletic Union. Betty Grable, then in the perennial co-ed period of her otherwise lustrous career, was his co-star. She might as well have been the Queen of England.

"She didn't know I existed," Luisetti acknowledges. "She was married to Jackie Coogan then and he was always on the set. I never talked to her, and when I was supposed to kiss her I couldn't bring myself to do it. It was horrible."

Luisetti's suspension was lifted for the 1940-41 season, and he led the San Francisco Olympic Club to the finals of the National AAU tournament in Denver. With Luisetti hobbling on an infected foot, the Olympians lost but he was the high scorer and most valuable player of the tournament. He played the following year with the Phillips Oilers, although a knee injury curtailed his usefulness.

Luisetti enlisted in the Navy after Pearl Harbor and was sent to the St. Mary's Pre-Flight school in Moraga, a town across the Bay from San Francisco. He may have played his finest basketball there. In 1943-44, his last season as a player, St. Mary's Pre-Flight went undefeated and Luisetti consistently outscored the other service stars, including Stanford All-America Jim Pollard, later a professional star with the Minneapolis Lakers. Howie Dallmar is among those who are convinced Luisetti was never better.

"We played St. Mary's Pre-Flight when I was a sophomore at Stanford," he says. "In the first game I got something like 23 points and Hank got 19. The papers started building up a rivalry between the old Stanford star and the new one. It scared me to death. I'd seen Hank play enough to know what he could do if he had to. I knew there was no way I could stop him. The next time we played them, Hank got 29 points. I got six."

In November 1944 Luisetti was marking time on a Navy base in Norfolk, Va., while awaiting sea duty aboard a carrier. On a cold, wet night he and several fellow officers decided to go to a movie in town. During the drive to the theater Luisetti complained of dizziness and nausea. He was dropped off at the dispensary, and that was the last thing he remembered for a week. He had spinal meningitis, a disease that until the introduction of sulfa drugs in the 1930s had been invariably fatal. He was in the hospital for four months, and when he emerged he was 40 pounds under his playing weight of 185. He was told by the doctors that he could never play basketball again. He was 28 years old.

Despite his medical history, Luisetti received professional basketball offers after the war but dutifully rejected them all. He went to work as a salesman for the Stewart Chevrolet Company in San Francisco and reluctantly agreed to coach the company-sponsored basketball team. In 1951 it won the AAU championship, the title that had eluded Luisetti and the Olympic Club a decade earlier. He quit coaching after that and never returned to the game.

Although there were "new Luisettis" popping up all over the map during the late '30s and '40s, his fame ended almost as abruptly as his coaching career. Tom Gola, the do-everything player for La Salle in the '50s, was the last man frequently likened to Luisetti. There are no "new Luisettis" today.

★ ★ ★

Jack Calderwood is white-haired and, because he stoops a little, probably shorter than he was when he was the rebounding "Spook" of the Luisetti era. Calderwood is a writer, and in researching a book on the young people of Sausalito, the hip little community across the Golden Gate Bridge from San Francisco, he spent hours each day in a waterfront hangout called Zack's. "They thought I was a narcotics agent at first, or at the very least a dirty old man. But after a while, they got used to me," he says. "I became a good rock dancer and was in some demand as a dancing partner. One day I learned that a member of the band playing there was a Stanford dropout, a former football player. I sought him out and explained that I had been an athlete at Stanford long ago. He was not really interested. Finally I asked him if he'd ever heard of Hank Luisetti. He just shook his head irritably.

"'Well,' I told the boy, 'if you haven't heard of him, I'd better tell you.' And I did, at length. When I had finished, it was the strangest thing. This boy, this rock musician, this college dropout, this modern person, was genuinely interested. I couldn't have been happier."

It Was Then
A Shanty Town

There is in a man's lifetime that precious moment when he knows he's got it made.

He's usually wrong, of course. But what matter?

I think my big moment came when I received my first Christmas card from Shanty Malone. I was barely of drinking age—though Lord knows I was an experienced tippler—so that the big green card served as testimony to my manhood. Besides Malone's was the most famous saloon in town at the time, and to be considered among his honored and regular customers was truly a badge of distinction.

I suspect Shanty dispatched about 50,000 or so Christmas cards in those days, so mine was hardly a signal honor, but I nevertheless felt myself to be among distinguished company that also included most of the big-name athletes in the community.

★   ★   ★

Shanty is reputed to have operated upwards of nine saloons in his 40 years of serving the city's thirsty, but I only patronized one of them, the green-windowed slum across from the Federal Reserve Bank on Sansome street.

I went there frequently as an undergraduate at Berkeley for at least three good reasons: (1) Shanty's offered the opportunity to rub shoulders and hoist glasses with sporting celebrities; (2) it was perfect for showing some naive little sorority girl how worldly you were; and (3) you could get a drink there after 2 a.m.

In fact, no college girl then extant could help but be impressed when you rapped on the Shanty door, muttered your name and were admitted to what was the biggest floating party in town. The police of that time, some 20 years ago, were not nearly so sensitive to the letter of the law.

But for all the pretense, I honestly liked Shanty's. If someone

88

were to reconstruct a modern bar in its image today, the owner could rightfully be called a phony. The dirty floors, the yellowed pictures of athletes on the wall, the Irish tenors singing at tuneless pianos would all seem a bit much.

★   ★   ★

Even the barroom brawls that occasionally marred the congeniality would seem staged today. But Shanty's was authentic, as authentic as the chaotic Irishman who was always there.

I had some memorable conversations at Shanty's, some of which I even remember. There was the time shortly after I'd returned from the Korean War—which I fought in Stuttgart, Germany—that I found myself seated alongside a burly, gray-haired man with cauliflower ears.

At the time I was much enamoured of Hugh McElhenny's running style, and at the drop of an ice cube I'd swing into what had become for my friends a familiar monologue.

My companion, I paused long enough to observe, made occasional references to "When I was playing." Finally, I asked him his name.

"Well, you probably never heard of me, son," he replied. "But I'm George Wilson."

"Not George Wilson of Washington, the great All-American by any chance?" I shot in.

★   ★   ★

He was the same, of course. And his reaction when I said I sure as hell had heard of him will stay with me for many years. He just clasped my hand and muttered, "Thanks." Then he added:

"By the way, on my best day I couldn't have carried McElhenny's shoes." Only he didn't say shoes.

Things like that always seemed to happen at Shanty's. In the retelling, they always sound contrived, but that's all right too, for Shanty's was somehow fictional.

Send in
The Clown

*Max Baer could bust them up with a right hand and
then break them up with laughter, but his boxing career
was overshadowed by tragedy*

He had few qualifications for his job. He did not emerge snarling
with resentment from a ghetto, nor was his childhood lost in the
bowels of some coal mine or steel mill. He was predominantly
German on his father's side of the family. Scotch-Irish on his
mother's, but no ethnic fires flamed in his far from savage breast.
Although in the latter stages of his boxing career he wore the Star
of David on his trunks, he was only a quarter Jewish, by virtue of a
paternal grandfather. He was reared on farms by parents so loving
that the children kissed them goodby before journeys no more ven-
turesome than to the town pharmacy. He was such a timid youngster that he refused to fight when challenged by his schoolmates,
sending forth his older sister as surrogate belligerent. By his own re-

collection, he did not hit another person until he was in his late teens, and then not in anger but in self-defense. Boy and man, he sought only to amuse. He seems, like Sabatini's Scaramouche, to have been "born with the gift of laughter and the sense that the world was mad." Above all else, he was a lover, not a fighter.

That such a man should have become heavyweight champion of the world and a principal in some of the ring's bloodiest conflicts, including one—purportedly two—that brought about the death of an opponent is one of the most remarkable paradoxes in the history of sport. In all probability, there has never been a fighter so contradictory in nature as Max Baer, and this is written with full knowledge that Muhammad Ali is equal parts jester and assassin. Forty years before Ali occupied center stage, Max Baer was entertaining and confounding ringsiders with routines that seemed more appropriate to musical comedy than to the squared circle. Unlike Ali, Baer was invariably the butt of his own japery, and if he was not the fighter Ali is—or was—he could, as they say, sure bust you up with a right hand.

Fighting at a time when only the most pedestrian of journalists addressed pugilists by their given names, Baer accumulated more nicknames than any fighter before or since. It is a tribute to this infinite variety that he was the Livermore Larruper, the Livermore Butcher Boy, Madcap Maxie, the Larruping Lothario of Pugilism, the Pugilistic Poseur, the Clouting Clown, the Playboy of Pugilism and the Fistic Harlequin. He provided lively newspaper copy, for he was the most quotable of boxers; in all likelihood, the most quotable of athletes. When ex-champion Jack Dempsey, working in Baer's corner during his fight with Joe Louis, advised him not to worry because "he hasn't hit you yet, kid," Baer turned dolefully to Dempsey and, through bloodied lips, replied, "Then you better keep an eye on Arthur Donovan [the referee] because somebody in there is beating the hell out of me."

Still, as many fans and newsmen as Baer delighted, he antagonized an equal number. For those who took seriously the most serious of all sports, Baer was outrageous. He had a magnificent 6'2½", 210-pound physique, with "airplane-width" shoulders, a broad chest, a 32-inch waist and long, smoothly muscled arms. He could take a punch as well as any heavyweight, and there are those who say he hit harder with a right hand than anyone who ever fought. When it was fashionable among fight people to sculpt in the imagination the composite boxer—Louis' jab, Dempsey's left hook, etc.—the right hand was invariably Baer's. But he seemed to do his roadwork on nightclub dance floors, and his sparring was mostly verbal. His training camps—in boxing tradition, hideaways as free of merriment as Montserrat—were like borscht circuit resorts, with Max as social chairman. Against the fiercest opponents he often fought indifferently and with the detachment of one reviewing a performance instead of performing. "Did the people enjoy it?" he would inquire after the battle.

In 1935 Baer lost his championship to the Cinderella Man, James J. Braddock, a 10-1 underdog, in one of the biggest upsets in ring history. He clowned through much of this desultory bout, grimacing in imitation of the movie tough guy, hitching up his pants, chatting amiably with ringside spectators. After one glancing Braddock blow, he performed a rubber-legged dance that Chaplin might have envied. All the while, the plodding, desperate challenger, fresh off the relief rolls, was collecting the points that would win him boxing's richest prize. As if the comedy in the ring were not enough, Baer would josh about the defeat afterward. Complaining that he had been literally handicapped—he had in-jured his right hand in training—he quipped, "My punches hurt me more than they did Braddock."

But there were occasions when Baer looked as if no man alive could survive in the ring with him. Max Schmeling was among the finest of heavyweights, an ex-champion, later the first conqueror of Joe Louis. On June 8, 1933, in the searing heat of Yankee Stadium, Baer knocked out Schmeling in the 10th round of a fight that earned the winner a chance at the title. Schmeling went down in that final round from a picture-perfect right that left him squirming on the canvas. He regained his feet, but the fight was quickly stopped. Baer won the championship easily, knocking down Primo Carnera 11 times in 11 rounds before the fight was halted. Even with so much on the line, he remained Madcap Maxie, remarking to the champion after he had been dragged down by him after an exchange, "Last one up is a sissy."

"Max hated fighting," says Mary Ellen Baer, his widow. "How he ever hit anybody, I'll never know. He wouldn't even strike his own children. All he wanted to do was entertain people. I can't imagine a person as soft as he was becoming champion of the world. He was so kind. He had no mean streak at all."

"He was one lovable bastard," says Tom Gallery, who promoted some of Baer's fights in the Los Angeles Olympic in the early '30s.

"He's the last person you'd ever expect to be a fighter. Why, he'd be clowning around 10 minutes before a fight. But, oh, what he could have been."

"It is incongruous that such a gentle, ingratiating man should have been a fighter," says Alan Ward, former sports editor of the Oakland *Tribune*, who was on the boxing beat at the start of Baer's career in the San Francisco Bay Area. "I remember when he was training for an important fight up at Frank Globin's resort in Lake Tahoe. My God, now that I think about it, it might even have been the early part of his training for Carnera. Anyway, he did about three weeks of pretty tough work. He had his brother Buddy with him and his trainer, Mike Cantwell. Max was actually working hard. This was for the championship, mind you. Then one night the phone in my room rang and it was Max. 'Let's go to Reno,' he says. I protested, but after all, it wasn't too far and I was a newspaperman, so I said O.K. Well, we hit some spots. Max wasn't much of a drinker, but he liked the atmosphere in the clubs. Word got out that he was in town, so he had an audience wherever he went. All night long he entertained, dancing and singing. At daybreak he was leading the band at one of the all-night places—I believe it might have been a brothel. All this while training for a big fight. When we got back to Globin's, there like the portrait of doom stood his trainer, Cantwell. Max went out and did his roadwork without saying a word."

The ring was Max Baer's stage. He was a farm boy who gloried in crowds, the lights, the action. The business of the ring, the actual fighting, was an intrusion to be gotten over with. Fighting was a means of making easy and quick money, and the farm boy coveted fast cars, fancy clothes and fast and fancy women. His career, 1929-41, exactly spanned the years of the Great Depression, a time when many a poor but strong young man turned in desperation to boxing as a livelihood. Boxers in the Depression were often the protagonists of plays and films, portrayed not so much as Neanderthals but as sensitive victims of the system. The fighters in *Golden Boy, City for Conquest, Here Comes Mr. Jordan* and even *The Prizefighter and the Lady,* featuring Myrna Loy and Max Baer, were not primitives. Before the seamier side of the business became exploitable dramatically, boxing could be made to appear the stuff of romance.

★   ★   ★

Baer discovered rather late in his youth that fighting was something he could do well. It did not immediately occur to him that a price for his prowess would be exacted. He would not pay in physical injury as so many others had, but in something dearer—mental anguish.

Max Baer was born Feb. 11, 1909 in Omaha. His father, Jacob, was a butcher of distinction, capable of dressing a 1,300-pound steer in three minutes and 36 seconds, a time he recorded in a contest in Denver, where the family had moved. When Max was in his teens, Jacob took the family to California, first to Galt, then to a hog ranch he had leased near Livermore, 45 miles east of San Francisco. There were four Baer children—Frances, the oldest, Max, Bernice and Jacob (Buddy), who would himself become a heavyweight contender. There was also Augie Silva, a Portuguese immigrant, a year younger than Max, who worked with the boys on the ranch and eventually took the Baer name as his own.

According to family legend, Max did not learn to fight until he was wrongfully accused of stealing a bottle of wine from a tough steeplejack in an argument outside a Livermore dance hall. The accuser popped teen-ager Max on the chin, and Max laughed, mostly, he said later, because he was glad he was still alive. When the steeplejack tried another punch, Max knocked him kicking with a single righthand haymaker. It was a heady moment for a boy who had believed himself a coward and, the Baers say, it was the making of a heavyweight champion. Encouraged by his family and friends, Max bought a punching bag for $25 in Oakland and set up a gym in an abandoned building on the ranch. With his newfound confidence and the conviction that the ring offered better wages than did slaughtering hogs, he sought counsel from the savants of "Bash Boulevard," a three-block stretch of Franklin Street in downtown Oakland where the fight crowd congregated.

"He looked like an Adonis," recalls Joe Herman, boxing's current elder statesman in the Bay Area. "But he was just a big inexperienced kid. Still, with that build, everybody wanted to help him." Baer's first bona fide manager was J. Hamilton Lorimer, once his employer at the Atlas Diesel Engine Works in Oakland. As a tutor, Lorimer hired Bob McAllister, a fistic classicist who, like Gentleman Jim Corbett before him, had represented the San Francisco Olympic Club as a heavyweight. Although his sensibilities were frequently offended by his wild-swinging proté gé, McAllister perservered with his lessons, contriving somehow to teach him a passable left hook. Baer made his professional debut early in 1929 with a second-round knockout of Chief Cariboo in Stockton. Fighting primarily out of that California valley city and Oakland, he quickly accumulated a string of 12 knockouts. He advanced from the Stockton rings to the Arcadia Pavilion in Oakland and to the even more capacious Oakland Auditorium. His first fight outside the Bay Area was a 10-round decision over Ernie Owens in Los Angeles on April 22, 1930. The victory itself was no more impressive than the contract-signing ceremony that preceded it. Baer arrived for this event in a limousine, driven by a chauffeur and attended by a footman. He stepped out of the car dressed as if riding to hounds. "I knew then," says Gallery, "that Max Baer was a little different from the ordinary guy."

Baer's reputation as a murderous puncher and *bon vivant* spread throughout California. He was now a drawing card, and his fight with Jack Linkhorn on May 28, 1930, transferred from the Arcadia to the Auditorium, drew a sellout crowd. Linkhorn, winner of 18 consecutive fights by knockout, was knocked out by Baer in the first round. The winner's purse of $7,500 was Max' biggest. He went through it in a flash, for even at 21 he was a prodigious spender. In later life this largess would assume the form of extravagant generosity; in these early years, he simply spent what he made on himself and his parents. He was frequently in debt, and to keep solvent he devised the ultimately pound-poor scheme of selling pieces of himself to various investors. When a final accounting was attempted to determine who owned what of him, lawsuits fairly fluttered through the courtrooms, some filed by Baer himself. But neither litigants nor creditors could daunt his high spirits. Baer moved his family off the hog ranch into a fine house in Piedmont where all the East Bay swells lived, and there were cars and clothes and girls by the score for him. He was the toughest man in town and the handsomest, a recognizable figure on the streets, a big, cheerful, curly-haired kid with a loud and infectious laugh.

At the same time, Baer was arousing the interest of men of stature in boxing, including Ancil Hoffman, a gnomish, tight-fisted avocado grower and fight promoter from Sacramento. What Baer needed, Hoffman concluded, was one more major local fight before tackling the Eastern promoters. He decided to match him with Frankie Campbell, a tough San Francisco heavyweight, in an outdoor bout on Aug. 25, 1930 at Recreation Park, home of the San Francisco Seals Pacific Coast League baseball team. Hoffman saw the fight as a bridge to the East. As it turned out, it was a plunge into despair.

Frankie Campbell, born Francisco Camilli, was an Italian from San Francisco's Glen Park neighborhood, the brother of a promising first baseman with the Sacramento Solons, Dolph Camilli, later, as a Brooklyn Dodger, the National League's Most Valuable Player. Campbell was a crowd pleaser, a busy mixer in the ring who had enjoyed recent successes in Los Angeles. In his last L.A. bout, he had been knocked down twice in the second round by Tom Kirby before he knocked Kirby out in the third. Campbell was not a big heavyweight, but he hit with authority and he was considered most dangerous when he seemed hurt, because his favorite tactic was playing possum. He and his wife Elsie were new parents, so, though his ambitions were not as grand as Baer's, he, too, looked forward to the big purse an outdoor bout promised.

Campbell had not looked good in training for Baer. The San Francisco *Chronicle*'s Harry B. Smith, visiting his quarters in the Dolph Thomas gym, wrote prophetically, "Frankie had better not leave himself as open to attack in the ring with Baer, for it may prove disastrous to him." Baer, too, had looked dismal in his sparring sessions. He always did. But in 1930, he was in superb condition and he knew, as Smith had written, that this was a make-or-break fight for him.

★　★　★

Campbell had appeared lighter in training than the 185 pounds his manager, Carol Working, had said he would weigh for the fight. In fact, he weighed only 179—to Baer's 194—and this aroused some speculation that he might have been ill before the fight. But his handlers insisted he was in top condition. At the weigh-in, both fighters were admonished by the State Athletic Commission to "keep fighting as long as the other man is on his feet."

San Francisco is seldom warm in August, particularly in the evening, when the afternoon fog has settled on the hills, but Recreation Park, at 15th and Valencia Streets, was situated in the relatively wind- and fog-free Mission District, then as now, the best place in town to watch sports outdoors. "Old Rec," as the ballpark was called, had been built of lumber and chicken wire in 1907, the year after the great earthquake and fire, and when the wind blew, it creaked like a fence gate. By 1930 it was considered obsolete. The following year the Seals would move into the modern Seals Stadium, so that the Campbell-Baer fight would be one of the last major sporting events to be held there. A crowd of between 15,000 and 20,000 showed up on an unseasonably balmy evening to watch the two young heavyweights.

Campbell was the aggressor in the first round, eluding Baer's right hand and scoring with his shorter, crisper punches. Near the end of the round, however, Baer dropped him with a looping right to the jaw. Campbell took a count of nine and did not seem seriously hurt. In the second, Campbell stung Baer with a left to the ribs and Max went down. He protested to Referee Toby Irwin that he had merely slipped, and Irwin agreed, motioning him back into action. Campbell, meanwhile, had not retreated to a neutral corner, as he would have been required to do in the event of a knockdown. Instead, he had strolled to the ring ropes and, inexplicably, began staring out at the crowd. As Baer regained his feet, a photographer's flashbulb exploded in his eyes, momentarily blurring his vision. He said later that Campbell appeared to him as only a shadow figure. Campbell was still gazing abstractedly as Baer advanced on him. He turned just as Baer caught him with a right to the side of the head. The blow stunned Campbell, but he held on and survived the round. Between rounds, he was heard to confide to his second, Tom (Greaseball) Maloney, "Something feels like it broke in my head."

But Campbell fought well in the next two rounds, staying even in the third and clearly winning the fourth. He was ahead on some scorecards in the fifth when Baer, the right-handed slugger, surprised him with a whistling left hook to the jaw. Campbell slumped back into the ropes in a neutral corner as Baer, sensing his opportunity but wary of possum-playing, belabored him with a succession of powerful punches to the head. Campbell did not go down. He could not, for the ring ropes were supporting him. With his opponent still on his feet, Baer kept punching. One of the blows caused Campbell's head to smash against the metal turnbuckle that joined the ropes with the ring posts. Still, he did not go down. The furious assault could not have lasted more than a few seconds, but it seemed to ringsiders like minutes before Irwin stepped in and pulled the flailing Baer away. As he did so, Campbell slumped unconscious to the canvas. A count was unnecessary. As flashbulbs popped, Irwin held Baer's hand aloft, while Campbell's seconds worked frantically to revive him. Baer helped them carry him to his stool.

The photograph of Baer that appeared in the morning *Chronicle* showed him smiling as winners are supposed to, but it was accompanied by a story saying that, as of one o'clock in the morning, Frankie Campbell "lay in St. Joseph's Hospital still insensible." Dr. Frank Sheehy of the hospital staff told reporters the fighter had suffered extensive brain damage and that "the outlook is very dark." Smith's story of the fight portrayed Baer as a vicious fighter. "He [Campbell] was ready to drop, but Baer continued to rain in blows to an unprotected jaw and against a man who was already knocked out . . . Campbell was dead to the world and stayed in that unconscious condition as Irwin raised Baer's hand and posed for the picture of the winner."

After he had showered, Baer asked Hoffman if he might visit Campbell in his dressing room and wish him well. "Frankie isn't in the room yet," Hoffman told him. "He's still in the ring." In fact, Campbell lay in the ring for a full half hour after the fight while an ambulance from nearby Mission Emergency Hospital threaded through traffic to the ball park. Baer went to the family home in Piedmont secure in the knowledge he had won an important fight, unaware that his opponent lay near death.

Early the next morning Baer received a phone call from the hospital. Campbell was not expected to live, and the police were asking for him. Baer replaced the receiver and turned to his family. 'He just stood there, tears as big as golf balls rolling down his cheeks," Augie Baer recalls. "All the heart seemed to go right out of him then." Max had himself driven to the hospital, where he encountered Campbell's wife, who generously absolved him of blame. "It could have been you," she told him. He could barely speak in reply.

The fight officially ended Monday at 10:34 p.m. Frankie Campbell, age 26, died at 11:35 a.m. Tuesday of a double cerebral hemorrhage. Baer surrendered that afternoon to San Francisco Police Captain Fred Lemmon at the Hotel Whitcomb. The bail of $10,000, set by Superior Court Judge George H. Cabaniss, was the highest ever for a charge of manslaughter in San Francisco. Baer spent much of that day in jail before Hoffman arrived with the bail money.

The manslaughter charge was eventually and properly dismissed. That any such action should have been contemplated was in itself extraordinary, considering the circumstances of Campbell's death. Baer had operated within the rules of the prize ring. His opponent was still standing, and the referee had not stopped the fight. To quit punching under these conditions would have been to ignore the athletic commission's admonition. Still, Baer was vilified in the press as a dirty fighter. By striking Campbell from behind in the second round, an act that some were now—inaccurately—claiming was the beginning of the end, he had acted in an unsportsmanlike manner, the newspapers agreed. Working, Campbell's manager, insisted that Irwin should have declared his fighter the winner on a foul at that very moment. But Irwin had waved Baer back into action after his slip, and it was Campbell's responsibility, as it is every boxer's, to protect himself at all times. And if Campbell had been seriously injured by this "sneak punch," how was it possible, then, for him to have fought so effectively in the two succeeding rounds? And why hadn't Working thrown in the towel when his man was so obviously in trouble in the fifth, if he was so solicitous of his well-being? For the public, the fact remained that Baer had hit a man almost from behind and had continued to hit him when he was literally out on his feet. The affectionate nickname, Livermore Butcher Boy, derived from Baer's former vocation, now took on a sinister connotation.

Baer was also the victim of an atmosphere of hysteria, fanned vigorously by William Randolph Hearst's flagship newspaper, the San Francisco *Examiner*. Campbell was the second boxer to die in a San Francisco ring within a week. On the previous Thursday, Johnny Anderson, an 18-year-old in his second professional bout, died after being knocked out the night before in National Hall by Reinhart (Red) Ruehl. In a city with a proud ring history, dating at least to Gentleman Jim, boxing was suddenly in bad odor. The *Examiner*, which two years earlier campaigned unsuccessfully to abolish boxing in California, took up the cudgel again. An unsigned news story on the front page set the tone for a second—equally unsuccessful—anti-boxing drive: "The legalized prize-ring butchery, which the laws of California sanction under the name of 'boxing,' yesterday claimed another human victim, the second within a week."

Irwin testified before the athletic commission that Baer had acted within the rules and that he (Irwin) had moved as quickly as possible to stop the fight; Campbell's death was an unfortunate accident. The commission must not have agreed, because it suspended both Baer and Irwin for one year and for good measure, the managers and seconds of both fighters, nine persons in all.

To Max Baer the suspension was hardly the real punishment. That came from the terrible knowledge that he had killed a man with his fists. In newspaper accounts of his appearances in the courts and at Campbell's funeral, he was described as "white-faced," "trembling," a "ghost-like" figure with "lips pressed tightly and nervously together." He took up smoking. He suffered night-mares. He announced his retirement from the ring, only to be per-suaded by Hoffman, his manager to be, to take some time off and think things out. He had not killed anyone deliberately, Hoffman told him. It had been an accident, the kind that can happen in a business as brutal as prizefighting. But as a fighter, as a man, Max Baer would never be the same.

"Nothing that ever happened to me—nothing that can happen to me—affected me like the death of Frankie Campbell," Baer said after he had won the heavyweight championship. "It was almost a week after the fight before I could get more than an hour or so of successive sleep. Every slightest detail would come racing back to mind, and I couldn't blot from my eyes the last scene—Frankie un-conscious in the ring, his handlers working on him. And then the news that he was dying . . . dead."

Significantly, the severest criticism directed at Max Baer as a fighter in years to come was that he lacked the killer instinct required of great boxers. His son, Max Jr., recalls a conversation he had not long ago with one of his father's old opponents, Lou Nova. "Lou told me that my father hit him with the hardest body punch he'd ever taken. He said he was practically paralyzed there for a moment. But when he looked around, there was my dad, hitching up his pants, the way he always did, mugging away at the crowd, laughing, doing everything but follow up. Lou recovered and gave him a helluva beating."

"After Frankie Campbell," said Buddy Baer, "the clowning started. It was something to do instead of fighting."

Baer did not retire from boxing after the Campbell tragedy, but in his next few bouts he fought almost as if he had wandered into the ring by chance. His punches lacked power, and he seemed even less concerned than usual with protecting himself. He lost four of the next six fights. Ancil Hoffman, who had taken over as Max's manager two months after Campbell's death, commented in March, 1931, "I'm afraid the Campbell affair left its imprint on Baer, and that is something he will have to forget if he is to go far in the fight game. In all of his New York engagements Max failed to show the aggressive spirit that made him so popular on the Coast. I would say it affected his fighting considerably."

After the manslaughter charges were dropped, Max took Hoffman's advice and left for Reno, a favorite city, where the nightclubs and casinos never closed, the perfect place for a man who was barely sleeping at all. He gambled and drank a little, though never seriously, and he met a woman, one Dorothy Dunbar Wells de Garson of New York City, a sometime actress and frequent wife, then seeking divorce. She was pretty enough, though years older than Max, and, by his standards, chic and sophisticated. She charmed him and, to whatever degree was possible, helped free him of depression. But she could not make him fight well. She watched him lose to Ernie Schaaf in Madison Square Garden on Dec. 19, 1930, his first fight after Campbell. There was a grim irony in Schaaf being the opponent, for he, too, would die in the ring.

Baer's reputation as a fighter was scarcely damaged by the Campbell incident; indeed, fans in the Eastern arenas were clamoring to see so lethal a boxer. They were grievously disappointed to discover that the killer they had paid to watch was so tame he seemed afraid to throw a punch. The turning point came on Feb. 6, 1931, when Tommy Loughran, a master boxer, easily outpointed Baer in Madison Square Garden. Baer was so inept that ringside spectators began ragging him mercilessly, reviving at least the absent sense of humor. At one juncture in his hopeless pursuit of the elusive Loughran, he turned to a tormenting fan and shouted, "I'd like to see you try and hit this guy." Baer was so fascinated with Loughran's technical brilliance that he called on him in his dressing room after the fight to suggest they have lunch together the next day. Loughran, amused and flattered, accepted the invitation. Baer's trouble, aside from his curious reluctance to cut loose, was that he was looping his punches, Loughran told him. A clever boxer had no difficulty avoiding these tentative, telegraphed bombs. If he seriously contemplated remaining in the ring, Baer should forget about his past and learn a few basic skills. The man who could teach him most about shortening his punches happened to have refereed their fight. Fellow name of Dempsey.

The two fighters called on Jack Dempsey that very afternoon, and to Baer's astonishment, the old champion seemed interested in his plight. Baer was not on his way back yet—he would lose to Johnny Risko in May, to Paulino Uzcudun in July—but he acquired Dempsey as a teacher, and Hoffman was at last unraveling his tangled financial affairs. Dorothy Dunbar was attending to his heart, and she and Max were married in Reno on July 8, 1931. The marriage lasted barely two years, but Max was at least on his feet again. After Uzcudun, he won 12 fights in a row, six by knockout.

In Chicago, on Aug. 31, 1932, he fought a rematch with Schaaf, who was now a leading contender. It was a punishing, nearly even bout entering the 10th and final round. Neither man had been down; Schaaf, for that matter, had never been knocked off his feet in the ring. Then, five seconds before the final bell, Baer caught him with a long right to the chin, which he followed with a brief flurry of punches. Schaaf dropped to the canvas. Referee Tommy Thomas did not bother to count, declaring Baer the winner by decision, although Schaaf was still unconscious. Schaaf died six months later after being knocked out by Carnera in the 13th round at Madison Square Garden, felled by a punch so lightly thrown that ringsiders began chanting, "Fake!" as he lay mortally stricken. In footnoting Schaaf's death, *Ring* record books have long included the gratuitous phrase, "badly injured in his fight with Max Baer," the implication being that Baer had claimed a second victim. The killer reputation would not die, although the Carnera fight was Schaaf's fifth after Baer.

★   ★   ★

Baer fought only one time in 1933, against Schmeling, before 60,000 in Yankee Stadium. By this time, the 27-year-old Schmeling was being promoted as a personal favorite of the new German chancellor, Adolf Hitler. Schmeling was an athlete, not a politician, and a German, not a Nazi, but for the first time Baer pointedly wore the Star of David on his boxing trunks. The ring's ethnic scholars, including the late Nat Fleischer, never considered Baer a "Jewish fighter," a slight that rankled his Scotch-Irish mother, Dora. Exaggerating a bit, she told Bay Area reporters, "You can tell those people in New York that Maxie has got a Jewish father, and if that doesn't make him Jewish enough for them, I don't know what will."

This night it did not matter how much of him was Jewish. Normally friendly to a fault with all of his opponents, he regarded Schmeling as his first bona fide enemy. Weighing a svelte 203 pounds, Baer fought the fight of his young life. Still, in the first round he walked into a right hand that left him seeing more than one Schmeling. "I see three of him," he told Dempsey between rounds. The Manassa Mauler's sage counsel in reply is now part of ring lexicon: "Hit the one in the middle." Baer did and clinched a title shot.

Nineteen thirty-three was a vintage Baer year. The Schmeling victory had made him a national hero. Dorothy Dunbar divorced him in Mexico, leaving him free—actually, freer—to roam. He made *The Prizefighter and the Lady* and became an instant success with the Hollywood crowd. He was a *boulevardier*, a rake, a man about town. His love affairs were conducted on the grand scale. He was sued for breach of promise by an old girl friend, who told reporters she loved him so much she would "crawl on my hands and knees from Livermore to Oakland," a 35-mile journey over hilly terrain. A showgirl named Shirley La Belle accused him of making untoward advances in a New York hotel room. He was linked with June Knight, the Broadway star, and with cafe society ladies Mary Kirk Brown and Edna Dunham, the latter immortalized in the press as his "hotsy-potcha." Although Hoffman watched over his resources with a banker's eye, Max spent and gave away money as quickly as it was doled out to him. He would pass out $5 bills on skid row and buy and deliver groceries for poor families. "He'd beg Pop [Hoffman] for $250," Maudie Hoffman recalls, "then give it away to some down-and-outer waiting at the gate." "Max had a heart bigger than his body," says Buddy Baer. "He actually gave people the clothes off his back."

Early in 1934 he met Mary Ellen Sullivan, who managed the coffee shop in Washington, D.C.'s Willard Hotel. She was hardly a glamorous showgirl, but she was attractive, intelligent and level-headed, and he decided that he loved her. Despite vigorous objections from her Catholic family, they were married in June 1935. While he never quite lost his reputation as a playboy, they stayed happily married until the day he died.

Baer's training for Carnera was so nonchalant as to bring down the wrath of New York Boxing Commissioner Bill Brown, who, after discovering that the challenger's sparring sessions were more like soft-shoe routines, recommended that the fight be postponed until that "bum" could be made to take it seriously. But it was held as scheduled on June 14, 1934 in the old Madison Square Garden Bowl in Long Island City, which, curiously, had been the site of three heavyweight championship bouts, all of which the titleholder lost. The giant Carnera, mob manipulated and now abandoned, would be no exception. After Baer knocked Carnera out, Max turned to Commissioner Brown at ringside and inquired, "Well,

Mr. Commissioner, what d'ya think of me now?" "You're still a bum," snarled Brown. Then he considered the implications of his remark. "And so," he added, "is Carnera." From his dressing room, amid tumult, Baer called out, "Somebody bring the new champion a beer. Now I'm going out and have some fun."

Max Baer was heavyweight champion for one day short of a year, but it is unlikely anyone got more out of the title. One of his first acts was to fight a benefit exhibition—against Stanley Poreda— for Frankie Campbell's widow and son. A $10,600 trust fund was set up as a result of the bout, held on Feb. 15, 1935 at the Dreamland Arena in San Francisco. Baer paid all of the expenses and took no money from the gate.

His first defense of the title was to be against Braddock, a 29-year-old loser of 21 out of 80 fights who had been on relief only a few months before the championship bout and who borrowed $37 the previous Christmas to pay his children's milk bill. Baer was even more of a mystery than usual in training. His hands, always brittle, were more troublesome than ever, and it was said he was bothered by rumors that the Carnera mobsters had moved into Braddock's camp. Braddock won the title on June 13, 1935 at the accursed Bowl in a dreary match enlivened only by Baer's comedy turns.

Despite this humiliating defeat, Max would enjoy his richest pay-day only three months later in Yankee Stadium against the ring's newest sensation, Joe Louis. Baer's reputation may have suffered, but a crowd of 84,831 paid $932,944 to see Louis knock him out in four rounds. Baer's entire purse of $200,000 was placed in annuities by Hoffman, and this and subsequent investments provided the Baer family with a handsome income. There was no time for comedy in this brief, if profitable, encounter. Baer was decked twice in the third round, and when he went down again in the fourth, he stayed down, patiently awaiting the full count while resting on one knee. It was the act of a quitter, his critics said.

"Sure I quit," Baer replied. "He hit me 18 times while I was going down the last time. I got a family to think about, and if anybody wants to see the execution of Max Baer, he's got to pay more than $25 for a ringside seat . . . I'm not going to be cutting up paper dolls. I never did like the fighting game, and this proves it."

He was only a buffoon to boxing fans from then on, although he showed flashes of his old power. As late as 1940 he dropped a right hand on the chin of Pat Comiskey, a promising young contender, that knocked him flat. Comiskey got up and Baer went after him, but when he realized the condition of his opponent, he held his hands apart and implored Referee Dempsey to stop the fight. There would be no more Frankie Campbells on his conscience. Max reached his nadir in his grotesque fight with Two-Ton Tony Galento, billed cruelly as "The Battle of the Bums." Baer dutifully clowned as the brawling fat man charged him, but he also administered a sound beating, and Galento was unable to answer the bell for the eighth round. At the conclusion, Max wrestled with a dwarf who climbed into the ring.

✶ ✶ ✶

He retired after his second loss to Lou Nova, on April 8, 1941, and the following year joined the Army, serving three years as a physical instructor. He was at his happiest in the years after the war, turning at last to his true love—show business. He made movies, worked as a disc jockey and radio talk-show host, refereed occasionally and, for a time, had a nightclub act with Slapsie Maxie Rosenbloom, the former light-heavyweight champion who had fashioned a successful film career playing punch-drunk fighters.

Mostly, Max stayed at home in Sacramento, where he lived near the Hoffmans, and doted on his three children—Max Jr., now, at 40, an actor (Jethro in *The Beverly Hillbillies*) and film producer; Maudie and Jim. He was, as always, generous with his time and money.

Baer did not have to work, but he could not stay off the stage. Few of his films were consequential, and in the one that was, *The Harder They Fall*, a fictional version of the Carnera story, based on the Budd Schulberg novel, he portrayed a character totally unlike himself, a vicious heavyweight champion who took offense when the Carnera character, not he, was blamed for the death of the Schaaf character. *The Harder They Fall* is significant in film history as Humphrey Bogart's last movie. It was also Max Baer's.

On the morning of Nov. 21, 1959 Baer was shaving in his room at the Hollywood Roosevelt Hotel, preparing for some TV appearances that day, when he felt a sharp pain in his chest. He cut himself on the chin with his razor blade, and, alarmed as much by the sight of blood—which he abhorred—as by the pain, he stumbled to the telephone. "I need a doctor," he whispered. "A house doctor?" inquired the switchboard operator. "No, dummy, a people doctor." When the doctor arrived, Baer insisted that he had to telephone the studio and say he would be late. Finally persuaded to lie down, he suddenly turned ashen and called out, "Oh God, here I go." He was dead of a heart attack at 9 a.m. at age 50.

Max Baer left behind a legacy of love. On his eldest son's 21st birthday, less than a year earlier, Max had written him, "If God said to me at anytime, 'Max Sr., I must take your life so your dear ones can have health and happiness,' I'd kiss you all, if possible, and willingly go. You can't measure my love for you." Two weeks before his father's death, Max Jr. had written to his mother, "Sometimes I worry a lot about dad because he's still such a big kid at heart. He never really got off the farm, even though he made the top. He thinks just like a big kid and is the most gentle person in the world. . . ."

More than 1,500 people, including some of the biggest names in boxing, attended Baer's funeral at St. Mary's Cemetary in Sacramento. A few years later, Jack Dempsey, who had been a pallbearer, provided an appropriate epitaph: "There'll never be another Max Baer," he began. Then he paused and smiled in memory of so exasperating and delightful a friend. "And that's the way it should be."

Remember the Day . . .

Memory will muddle history.

A treasured old movie will seem banal when seen again years later. The old songs can become ridiculous—"Dance, Ballerina, Dance . . . " And old friends have a way of changing.

Still, the longest home run I can recall seeing was hit by Ernie Lombardi 19 years ago in the Emeryville ball park.

Oh, I know, that tumble-down relic was not exactly spacious. The right-field bleachers could be reached by leaning over, and it was only 325 feet down the left field line, where the clothing store signs were.

And Lombardi, 40 years old then and in his last year of baseball, was not the same man who twice led the National League in hitting.

But on this night he "caught ahold of one." In the long years since, I have seen Mays, Mantle, Aaron, Maris, Mathews, Howard —the game's muscle men—play. But I have never seen a ball hit harder than the one hit then.

★　★　★

There never was any question about it being a home run. The only doubt was whether the ball would ever come down. As it happened, it's flight was interrupted by a light standard outside the ball park. And if memory serves, as it seldom does, we in the grandstand could hear the great gonging sound when the ball, just seeming to rise, met the post.

Well, that was years ago. But I have never forgotten it.

Ernie Lombardi is 59 years old now. In February, he suffered a heart attack which left him bed-ridden for more than two months and which now confines him to short walks and brief expeditions into the garden of his Oakland home.

Until this season, he had worked as a sort of host in the Candlestick Park press box. It was a job he got when the Giants first came here in 1958.

★　★　★

"I called (Bill) Rigney then and asked him to give me something to do," Lombardi recalls. He had never done much but play baseball since his childhood in West Oakland. Out of the game and idle, he was prey to those twin assailants, ennui and despair.

The Giants offered him work at the pass gate or as a night watchman.

"I didn't want either of them. I could never have worked at the pass gate. I'd have let everybody in."

Finally, Rigney told him to show up on opening day. His job, he said, was to "Stand in the press box and watch the game. I couldn't believe it—I was bein' paid just to watch a ball game."

★   ★   ★

But it would pay anyone to hire Ernie Lombardi to "just stand around." He is among the friendliest of men, and shy as he is, he is a gifted anecdotist. He gave the press box needed atmosphere. He was worth the money.

For the first time in many years, Ernie Lombardi had to reject this year an invitation to play in one of those old-timer games that give this nostalgic sport a certain continuity.

"You get a chance in these games to see some of the older guys— Paul Dean, Bill Terry, Stan Hack, Joe Medwick and Bill Dickey, people I played with back in the thirties."

★   ★   ★

In one of these games, he and Dickey were the catchers on the same old-timer team. Lombardi opened the game, and, as it was agreed, started to pass his tools to Dickey after his one inning behind the plate.

"Bill just said to me, 'Ernie, you wouldn't mind going another inning, would you? I forgot my glasses.'"

Lombardi wore his glasses, as he told the story. His hair is silver, and he walks as slowly as legend says he once ran.

But no ballplayer can ever become old. Always, you can see out of memory's cloud, that big bat swinging toward the elusive target. Then . . .

The Cable Cars,
The Fog—
and Willie

In an era when players rarely evoke affection, San Francisco's Willie McCovey has become a civic monument. Indeed, in his 40th year, he has taken on a glowing patina

As Willie McCovey sat in the San Francisco Giants' clubhouse at Candlestick Park last Friday, blissfully contemplating the start of his 20th major league season, he was approached by a curious figure attired entirely in red. A mechanical monkey clutching cymbals hung from the intruder's neck, and in his right hand the man held a kazoo. "I have a telegram for Willie McCovey," he announced, heralding his arrival with a kazoo chorus. "Are you that gentleman?" McCovey identified himself, and the stranger, from

Grams-n-Gags Singing Telegram Service, began to warble, with simian accompaniment and more or less to the tune of *Seventy-Six Trombones*, "How d'ya do, Willie McCovey/the Riviera Rats have asked me here/to express best wishes to you. . . ."

McCovey exploded with laughter. "That's from my fan club in San Diego," he told his teammates at the ditty's conclusion. "I used to live on Riviera Drive when I was playing down there. The Riviera Rats were my neighbors." Because the Padres were the Giants' Opening Day opponents, was it not odd that he should be celebrated in song by San Diegans? "Oh, no, they're just good friends. They root for me wherever I am," McCovey said. "I have fans down there. Nothing like here, though. This is something special. There's nothing really like it." True. Remarkably true.

Not many professional baseball players today are actually *loved* by their fans. Admired, certainly; encouraged, naturally; respected, possibly. But loved? Not on your life. People just do not go around loving guys with $3 million, 10-year contracts. And players these days are rarely considered integral to the life of the community they supposedly represent. How can they be when they seem constantly to be talking about playing out their options and "getting the hell out of this lousy ball park to someplace where they'll appreciate me"?

What truly sets McCovey apart from the run of modern athletes, then, is not so much that, at 40, he is the oldest of major league regulars but that in a time when cynicism is rampant in the clubhouses he embodies the ancient virtues of love and loyalty. He recalls simpler times, older sentiments—Enos Slaughter weeping at the news that he had been traded away from St. Louis, Lou Gehrig sobbing out his farewell to the Yankee faithful. During spring training last month McCovey was having dinner in a Phoenix restaurant with two fans, one nearly 70, the other in his teens. Both the man and the boy were wrestling with the anomaly of McCovey's wondrous popularity in a city, San Francisco, that has hardly clasped its baseball team to its communal bosom in recent years. "Maybe it's because you're such a nice guy, Willie," said the older fan. "I think people sense that."

McCovey is not one for hasty responses. Among his good qualities is a penchant for thinking before speaking. And his speech itself is distinctive; though there can be no questioning his impressive masculinity, he has the vocal mannerisms of an elderly Southern black woman. Speaking softly, employing homespun phrases, he is reminiscent of Ethel Waters in *The Member of the Wedding*. He considered the older man's compliment for a moment, set his napkin aside and said, quietly, "I would rather be remembered as a decent human being than as a guy who hit a lot of home runs. I love San Francisco and the people of the Bay Area. I think people there consider me part of the city. San Francisco is identified with certain things—the bridges, the fog, the cable cars. Without bragging, I feel I've gotten to the place where people are thinking of me along those lines. I'd like to think that when people think of San Francisco they also think of Willie McCovey. It's where I want to be, where I belong. I hope the people there love me a little in return."

Do they ever! Traded to San Diego in 1974, McCovey returned home in triumph last season. When he was introduced with the rest of the Giants' starting lineup on Opening Day of 1977, he was cheered for a solid five minutes. When he stepped to the plate for the first time, there was another standing ovation. The applause continued all year long. It was an outpouring of affection unparalleled in the city's athletic history. And on Willie McCovey Day last Sept. 18, it achieved idolatrous dimensions. If McCovey harbored even the faintest doubt about his place in the life of the community, it was quickly dispelled by this love feast. Newspaper editorials extolled him, television news programs recapitulated his life story. Even academe joined the celebration with a paean composed for the San Francisco *Examiner* by San Francisco State University English professor Eric Solomon. "He has always been one of ours, as boy and man," the professor wrote of the player, "and he typifies San Francisco's ambiguous relationship to youth and age. . . . We all want to come to the edge of the Pacific, find success when young, and discover success again, gain another chance before it's too late. . . . In an era of hard, financially aggressive, contract-minded athletes, Willie McCovey seems free, kind, warm, the way we like to think of San Francisco itself, a bit laid-back, no New York or Chicago, cities always on the make. . . . Let New York have the brawling power of Babe Ruth, let Boston have the arrogant force of Ted Williams. Let us have the warm strength of Willie McCovey."

McCovey responded to this encomium with a splendid season. He hit 28 home runs, the most since he last played as a Giant. He drove in 86 runs and batted .280. He broke Henry Aaron's National League record for career grand-slam homers by hitting his 17th and 18th. He got his 2,000th hit. His 493rd home run put him in a 12th-place tie with Lou Gehrig on the alltime list. And because he had batted only .203 with San Diego and .208 with Oakland in 1976, he was named the National League's Comeback Player of the Year. It was the stuff that dreams are made of.

And now, at 40, he is prepared to do it again. "I can't rest on my laurels," he said after a strenuous workout at the Giants' spring training camp. "I have to approach this season the way I approached the last. People will be looking."

McCovey still hears it said that he is too old and infirm—he has arthritis in both knees and in his hips and is in more or less constant pain—to duplicate or even approach last season's feats. Such talk mildly irritates him—nothing severely irritates him—for, like many a middle-aged man of parts, he considers age merely a condition of the mind.

"A lot of it is up here," he says, tapping his hairpiece with long fingers. "An older player loses his interest before his body goes. I really think Willie Mays could've played longer. What he couldn't quite handle was coming down to the rest of the league from where he had been. He was so much above everyone else that it bothered him to know he wasn't still 10 times better than the rest of us. He couldn't handle that mentally, but he still had a super body when he quit. A guy who's been that good never really loses all of his ability. The only thing he does lose is his desire.

"The same thing that happened to Mays happened to Aaron, only Aaron let himself get heavy. This is where I feel I have the advantage. I still do the things that are necessary to stay in shape. My weight, about 220, has been the same for a long time. I haven't lost the desire yet. When I get to the point where I say, 'Aw, I don't need to do that,' then I'll know I'm in trouble. But this is all I ever wanted to do, all I'd ever prepared myself to do. People say I've made sacrifices to stay in shape, but I can't really call them sacrifices, because the so-called bad things in life don't interest me anyway. Staying out in bars all night is not my style. Oh, I guess I do a little of everything everybody else does. I just don't do as much. I was raised that way. When you first leave home, you start doing things you wouldn't do at home but, deep down, you know what's right."

✷   ✷   ✷

McCovey learned his moral code growing up in Mobile, Ala., the seventh of 10 children, eight boys and two girls. His father, Frank, a railroad man, was a church deacon, and his mother, Ester, ruled the brood with Old Testament authority. "We went to church every Sunday," says McCovey, "and nobody ever smoked in front of my parents, even when we were all grown up. Of course, I never smoked anyway." Willie grew to be the largest of the children and, curiously, the only one remotely interested in sports. He was anchor man on his high school mile relay team, a center in basketball and an end on the football team. There was no baseball at Central High, but McCovey and his friends played on the playgrounds of the Maysville district. Across town, two other Mobile youngsters, Aaron and Billy Williams, pursued similar athletic lives. The three would later account for 1,674 major league home runs, two Most Valuable Player awards and three batting titles.

McCovey's talents were first recognized by Jesse Thomas, a playground director in Mobile who acted as a bird dog for the Giants. With scores of other youngsters, including Orlando Cepeda and Jose Pagan, McCovey was invited to a Giant tryout camp at Melbourne, Fla. in the winter of 1955. "All the minor league managers in the system were there, and they'd watch us. We'd just choose up sides and go at it," McCovey recalls. Alex Pompez, a pioneer scout of Latin and black players for the Giants, was responsible for informing each player whether he would be signed to a contract or sent home. "You could tell if you'd made it or not by the way he looked," McCovey says. "I didn't think I'd impressed anyone that week, and when Pompez came into my room, sure enough, he had that look on his face. He watched me with sadness in his eyes and asked, 'Why you no hit?' I told him I guessed I was just too nervous. I was waiting for him to send me home when he said, 'For some reason, they're gonna sign you anyway.'"

And they have been glad ever since. After batting well over .300 in his first four minor league years, McCovey started the 1959 season in Phoenix and finished it in San Francisco. In 95 Pacific Coast League games, he hit .372 with 29 homers and 92 RBIs. The Giants summoned him, and on July 30, 1959 he made a major league debut that is still a topic of conversation among Bay Area baseball fans, most of whom say they were there that day in old Seals Stadium. Against future Hall of Fame pitcher Robin Roberts, McCovey went 4 for 4—two singles and two triples, one of which reached the centerfield backdrop on a searing line. To San Francisco fans, still flushed with pride over the team they had had only a year, the spectacular arrival of the tall youngster was occasion for civic celebration. McCovey became an overnight celebrity. His uneventful life story was dutifully printed in all the newspapers. National magazines sought him out. And he was incessantly interviewed on television and radio, often to the regret of the interviewers, because McCovey at 21 was not much of a talker.

Despite the boffo beginning, McCovey's future with the team was scarcely assured. The Giants already had a first baseman in Cepeda, and he, too, was immensely popular. He had been the National League's Rookie of the Year in 1958, a title McCovey was to earn with a .345 batting average in 1959. Bill Rigney, then the Giants' manager, remains convinced that if Cepeda could have been persuaded to move to the outfield, San Francisco would have won the pennant that year. But Cepeda had territorial rights he was reluctant to surrender. He did take an occasional turn in the out-field and at third base, but his play away from first was less than inspired. "I could see his point," says McCovey. "Why should he make a fool out of himself playing out of position. The thing is, we both couldn't be on first." So it was McCovey who moved to the outfield. He made the transition without complaint, even though he had never played in the outfield before. "I knew I wouldn't be a Willie Mays," McCovey says, " and anybody who saw me play there could tell that right away. But I learned. I think I played it adequately."

The dilemma of who's on first was not resolved until Cepeda was traded to St. Louis in 1966. McCovey would enjoy some of his finest seasons thereafter (he won the league's Most Valuable Player award along with the home run and RBI titles in 1969). Although McCovey and Cepeda were good friends, Willie's relations with the enigmatic Mays were much more complex. The premier ballplayer of his generation, Mays was never as fully accepted by San Francisco fans as Cepeda and McCovey were. There was too much of New York about him, and while the younger players appeared publicly about town, Mays was virtually invisible away from the park. And yet he craved attention and was frequently peevish when others, obviously less deserving, received it in his stead.

When McCovey joined the Giants in San Francisco, Mays seemed to regard him not as a protege but as a satellite. "He'd even take me along on dates with him. He'd drag me everywhere. I looked up to him. All of us did. He was such a great player. I found myself spending so much time with him that I was getting to be a lot like him. I was copying his ways. I knew that wasn't me. I couldn't go on like that, so I deliberately took myself away from him so I could create my own identity. Some people took that as feuding, but we've always been friends. I guess I was as close to him as anyone can be, but I don't think anyone can get real close to him. We're neighbors now. I live in Woodside and he lives in Atherton, but we hardly see each other."

McCovey was not the transcendent all-round player Mays was, but with his great reach he has always been an effective first baseman and he was—and still may be—one of the most feared power hitters the game has known. Gene Mauch, the Minnesota Twins' manager, has described McCovey as "the most awesome hitter I've ever seen." Indeed, standing at the plate, his left shoulder dipped, feet spread far apart, bat waving menacingly, he gives an impression of size that exceeds even the 6' 4", 220-pound reality. His home runs are majestic, for sheer distance the equal of any stroked by the legendary tape-measure sluggers—Ruth, Foxx, Mantle, Howard, Stargell, Kingman and Luzinski. His reactions may have slowed after 20 years, but the swing is as vicious and perfect as ever. McCovey was an early student of Ted Williams, in the days when the Red Sox were training in Arizona, and his swing is a slightly uppercutted copy of the Splendid Splinter original.

He should hit his 500th home run this spring, and if he can hit 20 for the season he will pass Eddie Mathews, Mel Ott and Ernie Banks on the National League home run ladder and reach third place behind Aaron and Mays. He needs only 36 RBIs to pass Mathews, who has 1,453, and advance to seventh place behind Rogers Hornsby in that category. Plagued throughout his career by a daunting assortment of injuries that have involved nearly every section of his elongated corpus—neck, shoulder, arm, hip, leg— McCovey has contrived, nevertheless, to string together some imposing seasons. In the six from 1965 through 1970 he averaged 37.6 homers and 106 RBIs. He drove in 126 runs in both 1969 and '70, hitting 45 and 39 homers and batting .320 and .289, respectively. He tied Aaron for the home run championship in 1963, when he hit 44, and won the title outright in 1968 and '69 with 36 and 45. He also won the RBI championship those two seasons.

His decline in recent years is, in his opinion, more a result of injuries and the Padres' insistence that he was only a part-time player than to any marked erosion of his skills. His performance last year would seem to bear him out. It dismays McCovey that after so many brilliant seasons he should now be famous outside the Bay Area only for his age, but he concedes that even that is an improvement over his former reputation as the man who ended the

1962 World Series so dramatically with a line drive to the Yankees' Bobby Richardson while the potential Series-winning runs died on second and third. His assured election to the Hall of Fame will not rest, it is reasonable to say, on either age or an out.

★ ★ ★

It is often said of McCovey by those who have known him through the years that he has never changed. He is as unaffected by stardom as anyone of his stature can be. He denies vigorously that he has ever been a superstar, ever been "on top of the heap." He loves jazz but, instead of listening to it after a game, he now prefers, at his relatively advanced age, to crawl into the whirlpool bath he has had installed in his new home. He was married in 1964, but only briefly, and he rarely sees his former wife and daughter. He seldom socializes with baseball folk, preferring the company of people with more varied interests. The once tongue-tied youngster is now an able and frequent speaker on the banquet circuit, an indefatigable promoter of his ball club.

Few love affairs have been as satisfactorily consummated as the one between McCovey and his fans on his "Day" last September. Smiling back tears before the microphone, McCovey seemed to be trying to thank everyone in the stands individually—Master of Ceremonies Lon Simmons feared he might actually succeed—but in the end it was, fittingly, his bat that did the talking. Struggling all afternoon to reward his followers with a home run, he was hitless when he came to bat in the ninth inning with two outs, the score tied and the winning run on third. He hit the first pitch thrown by Cincinnati's Pedro Borbon on a line to left center for a clean single that won the game for the Giants 3-2.

"I think Willie showed everyone today just what kind of an individual he is," said Manager Joe Altobelli. It was hardly necessary, because everyone there already knew what kind of an individual McCovey is. They just need reminding from time to time.

Ol' Who-Dat Gudat
Worth One Drink

There is this animated conversation raging two stools away at
Hanno's in the Alley. A big, black-haired guy is doing most of the
talking.

"What d'ya mean, you ain't heard of Marvin Doo-Dat Gudat,"
he is shouting. "Wilson," he addresses the bartender, "tell 'em
you've heard of Doo-Dat Gudat."

Wilson just shakes his head. It is obvious that it is time for me to
enter the fray, since I quickly recognize the big man's plight: he is
an old Pacific Coast League baseball fan and nobody knows what
he's talking about.

"Doo-Dat Gudat," I say solemnly, "was a rightfielder for the
Oakland Oaks. Stocky guy, batted left-handed, choked way up on
the bat, which he waved back and forth, back and forth."

The big guy looks as if he's just located his missing brother.

★ ★ ★

"Frenchy Uhalt," he cries out. "Maurice Van Robays, the Belgian
Bomber. Hugh Luby."

"Demon Damon Hayes," I return. "Brooks Holder, Emil Maihlo,
Showboat Billy Schuster."

The big guy is almost crying. "Let me stand you to a drink,
friend," he says. "I didn't think there were many of us left."

Maybe, with the changing population, there aren't. We are old
Coast League freaks. The names we know and treasure nobody has
ever heard of.

"Jack Salveson," I say to him. "Tricky Dick Gyselman, Kewpie
Dick Barrett, Bill Raimondi."

"Roy Nicely," he returns. "Ham-handed Tom Seats, Bob Joyce,
Smead Jolley, Buzz Arlett."

"Lou Novikoff," I reply, "The Mad Russian, God bless his soul."

"Ah," we say in chorus, "there were names in those days."

117

★ ★ ★

And so there were. Ballplayers sounded like ballplayers then. Now the rosters are filled with names you might read on a shingle. Jackson, Bando and Monday. Lanier, Hunt and Hart. Hmmpf!

"Cecil Garriott," *my new friend says by way of reopening discourse.* "Al A-1 Wright, Manny Salvo, Les Scarsella. And what was the name of that kid first baseman who was killed in the bus crash?"

"Vic Picetti," *I answer.* "Mission High. A phenom."

"Wilson," *says my friend, mourning once again the departed teen-age first sacker,* "do us again, please."

★ ★ ★

People are moving away from us now. His friends, weary of I-told-you-so's from the big guy, are involved in their own private conversation, something about wages and working conditions. We are oblivious to all this, caught up as we are in our own arcanum.

"Jake Caulfield," *I say by way of thanking him for the beer.* "Del Young, Ralph Pine Tar Buxton, Henry Cotton Pippen."

"Lloyd Christopher," *he says, brushing back a tear.* "Johnny Vergez, Cecil Dynamite Dunn, Wally Carroll."

"Joe Sprinz and Oggy Ogrodowski," *I come back.* "Ad Liska, Marino Pieretti, Italo Chelini."

"Jimmy Herrera," *he ripostes,* "Joe Brovia, Gussie Suhr, Ray Perry, the Little Buffalo. And who was that skinny kid with the glasses who played shortstop for the Oaks?"

"Bill Rigney," *I answer.*

"Oh yeah, yeah. Say, whatever happened to him?"

"He went up," *I say.*

★ ★ ★

Going up—to the majors—was a privilege granted only a few of our heroes. Out of sight, out of mind.

"Sad Sam Gibson," *my friend continues.* "Neil Sheridan, the Big Buffalo. Win Pard Ballou."

"Yes, and Frank Kelleher to you," *I reply, forcefully pushing myself away from the bar.* "But I really must go now. Thank you for your hospitality. Been nice talking with you."

"Yes," *he says gratefully,* "there's nothing like a good conversation to stimulate a person."

Reg-gie! Reg-gie!!
Reg-gie!!!

*His clobbering of L.A. and the record book with three
home runs propelled Reggie Jackson into a whirl that
touched all the bases*

It had been a nocturnal day, the dampness and gloom relieved
only by the lights in the office buildings, but now, at dusk, shafts of
sunlight separated the clouds. From the windows of Reggie Jackson's Fifth Avenue apartment the orange leaves of Central Park
could be seen glistening below. Jackson ignored this fleeting victory
of light over darkness. For him day and night had become indis-
tinguishable, so frenetic had been his pace, so numberless his
obligations during the previous 60 hours. He was sprawled on a
living room chair, apologizing for the bareness of his walls. "Most
of my paintings have already been shipped to California," he said.
"They're too expensive to be left here over the winter. How about
some wine. White or red? I'm going to have me a Heineken."

He looked for all the world like a political candidate after a hard day on the hustings. His tie was loose, and the knife-edge creases of his trousers were intersected with fresh wrinkles; he was coatless, and his vest was unbuttoned. Jackson insisted he was not tired, only dazed. He had been that way, he said, since the last of his record-tying three home runs had dropped behind Yankee Stadium's center-field fence in the sixth and, because of him, final game of the 1977 World Series, which New York won 8-4. All three of those homers were hit on the first pitch, and each hammered the Los Angeles Dodgers deeper into a hole from which they never emerged. Jackson, sipping his beer and smiling, recalled them with pleasure.

"Well, the first [a two-run shot in the fourth off Dodger starter Burt Hooton] put us ahead 4-3, so that was real enough. It was a hook shot into the stands. Before the second one [a two-run line drive in the fifth], I talked to Gene Michael [a Yankee operative in the press box] and asked him what Elias Sosa threw. I knew I was going to hit the ball on the button after hearing from Gene, but I didn't know how quick it would come. That one iced the game 7-3. Before the last one I saw Charlie Hough warming up. A knuckle-baller. Frank Robinson taught me how to hit that pitch in 1970 when he managed me in winter ball. I thought if I got a decent pitch I could hit another one out. Anyway, at that point I couldn't lose. All I had to do was show up at the plate. They were going to cheer me even if I struck out. So the last one was strictly dreamland. Nothing was going through my mind. Here it's a World Series game, it's going all over the country on TV, and all I'm thinking is, 'Hey man, wow, that's three.'"

Jackson broke or tied eight World Series batting records against the Dodgers. His three home runs in the finale tied him with Babe Ruth for the most hit in a game, and they were the most ever hit consecutively. His Series total of five homers was another record, and with a home run in his final at-bat in the fifth game and a walk in his first plate appearance of the sixth game, he hit the most consecutive homers in more than one Series game. He had the most total bases in a Series, 25, and tied the record for most in a game (the sixth), 12. He scored the most runs, 10, and equaled the most in a game (again, the sixth), four.

At the end of Game 6 his teammates flocked to Pitcher Mike Torrez, who had pitched his second complete-game victory of the Series, and Jackson sprinted in from right field, dodging and bowling over the spectators, who had flooded on the field, like an NFL running back. He hardly stopped running for the next several days. For more than two hours after the final game he stood before his locker, entertaining and supposedly enlightening wave upon wave of newsmen with his philosophy, his theology and his analyses of the war-torn Yankee season, all the while quaffing champagne and exchanging pleasantries with those of his friends and teammates—they are not necessarily the same—who could get within shouting distance.

Jackson is beyond argument the top media draw in baseball. The space around his cubicle after even far less consequential games looks like the site of a crap game or a rugby scrum. Journalists are attracted to him not merely because he is dramatic and—that word again—controversial, but also for the even more basic reason that he is both willing and able to talk. Those of his colleagues who are less voluble and articulate, and that would include virtually all of them, smolder with resentment, like Cinderella's stepsisters, over the attention heaped on this media darling. It is a cross Jackson cheerfully bears.

He departed the Yankee clubhouse "about half crocked" on champagne sometime after two in the morning. He was driving his Volkswagen down Second Avenue, headed for a favorite saloon, Arthur's Court, when, he says, he observed the Honorable Hugh Carey, governor of New York, emerging from a place at 74th Street. Jackson stopped to chat, and they agreed to continue their discourse at the Jim McMullen bar two blocks away. "We talked till five in the morning," said Jackson, unimpressed by this revel with the state's chief executive. "Mostly about kids."

Jackson, wobbly but still game, sped home to shower and change clothes. At 6:30 a.m. he was standing at a slight lean before the *Today* show television cameras. Then it was back to the Stadium, where he and those of his teammates still functioning and in the proper humor assembled for a ticker-tape parade up Broadway to City Hall, where Mayor Abe Beame read a proclamation declaring Wednesday, Oct. 19, New York Yankee Day. There, Joe DiMaggio, who had thrown out the first ball of the climactic game, prophesied a new Yankee dynasty. Considering the number of Yankees who say they wish to play elsewhere, the old Clipper's vision of a new ruling family seemed no more reasonable than Dodger Manager Tommy Lasorda's claims of access to a Big Dodger in the Sky. When Jackson was asked by a newscaster after the reception what his plans were, he replied with uncharacteristic brevity, "I'm going to bed."

But he did not. He visited friends at the plush Cartier jewelry store, picked up his Rolls-Royce at the Stadium, bought some newspapers to confirm his own greatness, took a 45-minute bubble bath, watched television with the sound off, had dinner and retired finally at midnight after 40 hours of being more or less on his feet.

A better-rested Jackson entertained small clusters of visitors in his apartment for most of the following day. He did go out to receive the Series MVP award at the Plaza Hotel. Walking to his car after the ceremonies, he found that he required the services of policemen to escape mobs on the sidewalks. "Before the Series they would just stop and stare," Jackson said. "Now they come right up. They're polite enough—not too many backslappers—but I could've been there all day signing autographs."

His performance in the Series did not, he felt, balance out the strife he endured during a season that had him variously at odds with his teammates, his manager and the fans. "No, it's more a relief," he said. He leaned back in his chair as if to demonstrate the point. "I feel almost let down now. I realize that a lot of what happened I brought on myself. When you get so much money, a lot is expected of you. There are too many numbers involved with the Yankees. You take the economic situation in the country, the city being bankrupt, and here we are, the pinstripers, the money men. Little things we did and said became major. To me I'm just another person. It confuses me when people get all hyped up over what I do. There are 800 million people in China who don't give a damn. But I feel happy about what happened. I feel a great strength. I feel good for the people who stuck by me. I feel happy for the kids who can see that I made it back after all those odds against me. It was hard enough earlier. Just think what it would've been like if I hadn't performed."

Jackson took a long pull on his beer. "Sure, I'll be a Yankee next year. I'm a Yankee mainly because of George Steinbrenner. I'll continue to be one because of George Steinbrenner. But I'll say this, if things aren't better next year, I'll quit. No, that's not quite it. I just don't know if I can take it, that's all. But how can things not be better next year?"

Some friends dropped in, notably the Rev. Jesse Jackson, the Chicago civil rights activist. Reggie asked them to wait in the dining room while he finished talking about himself. He was going home to his Bay Area condominium in a few days, and he was looking forward to seeing his neighbors again, his old friends, some girls and his cats. This business of his requiring fan adulation is, he snorted, so much nonsense. He likes smaller groups, not adoring crowds.

Reggie left the room to pour some more wine for his other guests. Rev. Jackson stepped into the room. Like Reggie, he is a large, broad-faced, mustachioed man. The two Jacksons look enough alike to be brothers, which they are not.

"Because of his intelligence and his gifts, Reggie's domain is bigger than baseball," said Rev. Jackson. "All the bad pitches to him do not come on the diamond. He is a fascinating man. He has a sense of history, which so many athletes don't have. I think that's why he gets up for the big games. He has a sense of moment. Greatness against the odds is the thing. Anyone can be famous. Just by jumping out of one of these buildings you can be famous. To be great is a dimension of the authentic."

Reggie came back into the room, looking authentic enough. "Hey, you don't have to go now," he said to some guests preparing to leave. "Sit down. Have some wine. We'll talk a while."

Ronnie and Harvey Revisited

I am indebted to Lee Grosscup, the Oakland Raiders' publicist and retired itinerant quarterback, for reviving The Fantastic Saga of Ronnie and Harvey Knox.

And as Grosscup, in casual conversation, recalled their incredible career, it occurred to me an entire generation of Americans may have come to maturity in ignorance of this Dynamic Duo.

It would be criminal to permit an oversight of this magnitude to lie unattended. So with your indulgence, I'll tell the story.

The Knoxes first started happening in 1952, when Ronnie completed 27 touchdown passes for Santa Monica high school and became, in that cynical time, collegiate football's most ardently pursued property.

But the real beginning was eight years earlier, when Harvey, a onetime private detective and bar owner, married Ronnie's divorced mother and, stirred by memories of his own orphaned boyhood in Arkansas, told his nine-year-old stepson he'd see to it the boy had all the advantages step-dad never had.

★ ★ ★

No father was ever truer to his word.

Unfortunately, Harvey's paternal concern bordered on mania, and in the succeeding years few who had dealings with his stepson escaped his displeasure.

It took Harvey three years, for example, to find a high school football coach who could meet his exacting specifications. As a result, Ronnie was transferred from Beverly Hills to Inglewood to Santa Monica high schools, an odyssey uncommon even by Southern California's nomadic standards.

But Harvey did think highly of Santa Monica's Jim Sutherland, a coach who shared his dedication to the passing game—Ronnie's game.

124

Harvey thought so much of Sutherland, in fact, that the coach accompanied Ronnie the following year to the University of California campus in Berkeley in what the player himself later referred to as a package deal.

Harvey's selection of Cal was not made cavalierly, of course, for there were more than 30 schools bidding for the services of a boy whom Frank Leahy called "the finest high school quarterback I've ever seen."

★   ★   ★

Harvey made no secret of his attempts to locate his boy in an institution that would appreciate such rare gifts.

One of the college coaches interviewed by the agent-stepfather later said he was advised by Harvey to "give it to us cold. Just put your real offer on the line, and we'll tell you how it matches with the others."

Harvey soon learned that remarks of this nature earned him column inches in the newspapers. It was a lesson he never forgot.

In fact, by the time he had completed his investigation of the nation's system of higher education, Harvey had succeeded in making a travesty of the proselytizing game then in vogue.

It was, however, a game Harvey also played, for he was soon to reveal that part of his "deal" with Berkeley alumni involved recruiting services in Southern California for which he was handsomely remunerated. The offending alumni group, the Southern Seus, was eventually reprimanded by the Pacific Coast Conference.

★   ★   ★

Ronnie, meanwhile, became the star of the California freshman team. But in spring training the following year, Harvey, a constant visitor to the practice field, discovered to his horror that his boy was playing behind Paul Larson at quarterback.

"I'm not going to tell the California coaching staff how to run the team," he announced ominously. "But football is also my business."

Trouble, quite obviously, was ahead. Since Harvey had, at self-proclaimed personal sacrifice, dedicated himself to furthering his boy's athletic career, he had no choice but to voice protest.

The California coaching staff, he concluded, must be myopic in the extreme not to recognize Ronnie's limitless talent. Only two years earlier, after all, the boy had been the Nation's most coveted high school player.

★   ★   ★

In addition, not enough responsibility was being delegated to

Ronnie's high school coach, Jim Sutherland, who, by the merest coincidence had accompanied him to Cal the year before.

And the school had not fulfilled its alleged promise to provide Ronnie, a potential writer-actor, with newspaper and television work in the area.

So it was time to move on, an experience not uncommon to the Knoxes, since Ronnie had attended three Southern California high schools in search of a proper coach.

★   ★   ★

"We came to Berkeley on top and we're leaving on top," said Harvey. And as Bay Area sports fans gasped in shock, the decade's most publicized high school player withdrew from Cal and enrolled in rival UCLA.

"Ronnie," said his stepfather, "must be near the motion picture studios."

"His loss could hurt us," philosophized Cal coach Pappy Waldorf, "but perhaps we'll be better off in the long run."

Ronnie wasn't. Because of the transfer, he missed a year of eligibility at UCLA, and the following year, he missed much of the season due to injuries.

Furthermore, Harvey wasn't getting along with Bruins coach Red Sanders any better than he had with Waldorf.

★   ★   ★

When Sanders accused Harvey of bypassing the team physician to have Ronnie treated by the family doctor, the stepfather declared:

"It's time for coach Red Sanders to decide to have all this stuff cut out or Ronnie and I are going to be forced to make a serious decision of our own."

That decision was not long in coming, for in August of 1956, Harvey announced his stepson had signed a $25,000 bonus contract with the Hamilton Tigers Cats of the Canadian Professional Football League.

In three years of college—two colleges at that—this most celebrated of high school stars had played little more than half of one varsity season. Now he was a pro. But not for long.

★   ★   ★

Harvey called Hamilton coach Jim Trimble "stupid" for not playing the inexperienced quarterback often enough, and Ronnie was indefinitely suspended.

He played the rest of the season with the Calgary Stampeders, then was signed the following year by the Chicago Bears—and suspended after Harvey, complaining that Ronnie was being shortchanged in exhibition games, called coach George Halas a "skunk."

The next stop was Toronto, where Ronnie finally quit the game for good in 1959, opining that "football was for animals."

Ronnie and Harvey have since parted, Ronnie to pursue a career as a writer and actor, Harvey to real estate.

"It's simply a matter of evolution," Ronnie advised the press at the time of the split. "You've got to grow up sometime."

A Melding of Men All Suited to a T

Clark Shaughnessy was a dour theoretician,
Frankie Albert an unrestrained quarterback
and Stanford a team of losers, but combined they
forever changed the game of football

"There are no longer any distinctive systems in football. They've
become standardized. Nobody sees a balanced line anymore except
at Notre Dame, and even some Rockne-trained coaches are getting
away from it. There is only one formation that's any good and it's
the single wing."—Michigan Athletic Director and former Coach
Fielding H. (Hurry Up) Yost
on the eve of the 1940 college football season

"That hocus-pocus which is called the T-Formation made 90,000 spectator converts and seemed definitely to signal the arrival of a new era in college football. The day of the tug-of-war is out—Clark Shaughnessy and his Stanford Indians have definitely killed it."
—Curley Grieve, writing in the San Francisco Examiner
after the Rose Bowl game of Jan. 1, 1941

"The whole season was like a fairy tale."
—Frankie Albert,
quarterback of the 1940 Stanford team

The hiring of Clark Shaughnessy as football coach at Stanford for the 1940 season struck most alumni, fans and critics at large as an act of folly comparable to employing an arsonist as fire chief. In 1939 Stanford had won but one game and had been disparaged as the worst team ever to represent the university, but compared with the University of Chicago team Shaughnessy had coached that same season, Stanford seemed a veritable juggernaut. In 1939 Chicago had been beaten 85-0 by Michigan, 61-0 by both Ohio State and Harvard, 47-0 by Virginia, and 46-0 by Illinois. Chicago had scored just 37 points in eight games while 308 had been scored against it. At the behest of Chicago's president, Dr. Robert Hutchins, who detested the game, the university discontinued football after this mournful season. "I did not de-emphasize football at the University of Chicago," Dr. Hutchins boasted. "I abolished it."

Shaughnessy could have stayed at Chicago as a professor of physical education, but after 25 years as a coach he found the prospect of a fall without football insupportable. He was unquestionably available, but how, outraged Stanford alumni protested, could a man with such impeachable credentials be expected to lead the Indians out of the gridiron wilderness? The fact that Clark Shaughnessy did it so spectacularly is achievement enough, but he accomplished much more by the end of the 1940 season. In coaching Stanford to its only undefeated and untied record, he also contrived to change the game itself as radically as Einstein changed conventional thinking on physics.

Before Shaughnessy at Stanford in 1940, the T formation was a relic from football's antiquity. No one used it. Shaughnessy himself had not used it at Chicago, but he had experimented with the alignment as a member of the Chicago Bears' T brain trust, along with Owner-Coach George Halas and former Bears Coach Ralph Jones.

The Bears were the only professional team to run out of that arcane formation. The T had been used by Amos Alonzo Stagg at the University of Chicago before the turn of the century, but it was soon supplanted by the Pop Warner double wing, the Notre Dame box and the power-oriented single wing. With the success of these formations, the T seemed no more effective than the flying wedge, from which it sprang. Direct passes from center to a running back or passer protected by cordons of blockers represented the standard offense.

No one was prepared for the Shaughnessy T with its lightning thrusts and deception. An entire generation of coaches and players had grown to maturity without seeing the T, and no one had ever seen a T that placed such emphasis on wide-open play, for even under Stagg the formation had been built for power.

After Stanford's milestone performance in 1940, coaches turned to the T as if it were a revealed truth. By the end of the decade, according to a survey by *Football Digest*, 250 of the top 350 college teams were using it. Everyone, as the newspapers of the time were so fond of reporting, "was going to a T party." Even Frank Leahy flew in the face of all that was sacred and discarded the Notre Dame box for the T within two years of Stanford's epochal season. Now there is scarcely a team at any level of play that does not use the T in one form or other. Be it pro set, power I, wishbone or veer, it is essentially the same formation Shaughnessy introduced 37 years ago to an extraordinary group of young men who would become known as the Stanford "Wow Boys."

Shaughnessy's meeting with these players stands as one of those rare instances in life when time, place and personalities join in perfect union, when disparate and formerly malfunctioning parts mesh into a precision instrument. American football has never had a moment quite like it.

★   ★   ★

Clark Shaughnessy was 48 years old when he moved from Chicago to Palo Alto with vague hopes and volumes of unused play diagrams. From what he had seen on film of Stanford's calamitous 1939 season, he suspected that the material for the new kind of football team he envisioned was at hand.

When Stanford began its search for a successor to the deposed Tiny Thornhill, the talent scouts were surprised to learn in what special regard Shaughnessy was held by his coaching colleagues. For a man who had enjoyed only occasional success at Tulane,

Loyola of New Orleans and Chicago, he was looked upon as a sort of mad scientist who might yet rule the football world if his experiments could ever be made to work. The notion of hiring such an eccentric was not without appeal at a university that prided itself on innovation.

True, Shaughnessy's Spartan life-style seemed a bit severe for the West Coast. It was his practice to go to bed as early as seven o'clock of an evening and arise, chipper and refreshed, at three or four in the morning, ready for work. To the lasting grief of his subordinates, it was his conviction that they, too, should observe such a regimen. Shaughnessy neither drank nor smoked and looked upon those who did with disfavor. "When he said, 'Let's go have a drink,' he meant, 'Let's go drink a milk shake,'" recalls Marchie Schwartz, Shaughnessy's backfield coach and his successor as head coach. "He disappointed a lot of newspapermen that way."

Shaughnessy proved to be extremely sensitive to criticism, so his relations with the press would never be defined as warm, milk shakes or no. At one meeting of the Northern California Football Writer's Association, he demanded that an offending columnist leave before he would consent to speak. The meeting was abruptly adjourned. At a time when coaches were as much public relations men as field bosses, Shaughnessy held himself apart; he was an ascetic among hucksters. Roger Treat, the football historian, said of Shaughnessy when he later joined the Bears' staff full time, "I always looked upon Clark Shaughnessy as a conscientious idealist who might better have followed the trail of Father Flanagan of Boys Town. He may never be entirely happy in the jovial thuggery of pro football where every man has a little assassin in him." "The world," said Coach Bob Zuppke of Illinois, "lost the greatest undertaker when Clark Shaughnessy decided on football coaching."

Shaughnessy was so addicted to theory that he may have looked upon his players more as X's and O's than as flesh and blood. It was a failing that would eventually bring him to grief. He frequently did not recognize friends or acquaintances on the street, so preoccupied was he with the diagrams spinning in his head. When an interviewer asked him, innocently enough, what his hobbies were, Shaughnessy tartly replied, "Hobbies? Why, football is my hobby." Chuck Taylor, Wow Boys guard and later both football coach and athletic director at Stanford, has said he was never certain Shaughnessy knew his name on the field. "He knew my position and everything about it and he knew my jersey number, but my name . . . I just don't know."

Not only was Shaughnessy's appointment as head coach regarded with suspicion by some influential Stanford alumni organizations but it was also viewed with outright hostility. Their favorite candidates had been Dud DeGroot, an alumnus who was coaching just down the highway at San Jose State, and Buck Shaw, who at equally proximate Santa Clara University had taken two teams to the Sugar Bowl. Why had the university reached so far beyond the fence for a bad apple when it had two plums in its own backyard?

It was even suggested in some quarters that Shaughnessy had been hired to preside over the demise of Stanford football. Had not his previous employers, Loyola and Chicago, both dropped the game? "If the school is really going to deflate football," one alumni chapter cutely advised the Stanford Board of Athletic Control, "then there is no need of assisting in any way the athletes in the fold." The alums were not about to foot the funeral expenses.

For its part, the Bay Area press looked upon Shaughnessy's hiring as an occasion not so much for dirges as high hilarity. Stanford, that pillar of academe, had quite obviously made a fool of itself. Columnists Prescott Sullivan of the San Francisco *Examiner* and Jack McDonald of the *Call Bulletin* proposed that since the austere coach apparently had no nickname, he be called "Soup," the diminutive, they insisted with sledgehammer irony, of "super." Sullivan, cleverest of the local sportswriters, delighted in reminding his readers of Chicago's losing scores in 1939, protesting all the while that doing so was against his principles and in the worst conceivable taste. "We have heard it said," he wrote, "that Shaughnessy has developed the knack of losing to the point where, with him, it is an exact science. In light of his record, we aren't at all surprised at this."

If Shaughnessy was a certified loser, so then were the players he inherited from the benighted Thornhill, a coach who had achieved the heights with the "Vow Boys" Rose Bowl teams of the mid-'30s (so called because they vowed never to lose to USC, which they did not) but who had fallen into disgrace in 1939. Thornhill had reason to believe he was about to receive the Stanford ax when, with his team trailing Dartmouth 3-0 in New York's Polo Grounds, he reluctantly stepped forward to deliver his final halftime address of the 1939 season. It would be, in fact, his last halftime address ever. As he stood there before his downcast charges, it occurred to him that words were inadequate to express his displeasure, so he turned to his assistants for succor. They, too, were speechless. Finally, he called upon Bones Hamilton, a star Vow Boys halfback who had traveled with the team for the last game of the season. Hamilton did have something to say: "You are by far and large the worst group of players who have ever worn the Stanford red."

Stung by this depressingly accurate appraisal, the players rallied to score 14 points in the second half and win their only game of the season. Says Tackle John Carl (Jack) Warnecke, now an internationally renowned architect, "That was the making of the 1940 team."

The hero of that solitary victory was a left-handed, 170-pound tailback who had wavered between first and third string all season and who seemed, in fact, to be facing extinction under the grueling demands of the single and double wing formations. Frankie Albert had led Stanford's 1938 freshman team to an undefeated season but he had been inconsistent in his first year with the varsity. Still, of the seven touchdowns Stanford scored in '39, he had passed for four and run for two. As a boy growing up in Glendale, Albert had seen the Vow Boys play in Pasadena and had followed the adventures of USC Scatback Cotton Warburton in the Coliseum. Like Warburton, he insisted upon wearing jersey No. 13, although when he had first reported for football at Glendale High School the coaches could find no uniform, bearing whatever number, small enough to accommodate his 118 pounds. Albert played lightweight football for two years, then, at a strapping 145 pounds, led the varsity to the Southern California high school championship in 1937, his senior year.

Portentously, the winning touchdown in that title game against Santa Barbara High was scored on a play Albert concocted in the huddle. A certain passion for the unexpected would characterize his careers in both college and professional football. The playbooks, even Shaughnessy's thick folios, would never adequately cover the problems he was able to perceive. Even when Albert was going by the book, he appeared to be making up plays on the spot, for he had a habit of standing apart from a huddle and reconnoitering the enemy before rushing dramatically back to his waiting teammates as if seized with sudden inspiration. It was part of the Albert mystique. There have been better quarterbacks, but none with more flair.

Albert was as disheartened as his coaches were by his erratic performance in 1939. "I guess I'm just another of those high school players who can't develop enough for college football," he told his brother Ward.

★   ★   ★

The losers, coaches and players, met for the first time in March of 1940 in a history classroom on the Stanford quadrangle. The players instantly recognized comic possibilities in this marriage of misfits. "We'd been reading about all those beatings Shaughnessy's team had taken," recalls Fullback Milt Vucinich, now a successful San Francisco businessman, "so we were joking among ourselves that wasn't it just like Stanford to hire somebody like this to coach us." Says Warnecke, "We felt Shaughnessy was only what we deserved."

The sardonic laughter was abruptly squelched when Shaughnessy strode through the classroom door. Standing before them, his back to a large blackboard, he was hardly what the players had expected. A man who could absorb 85-0 beatings should be slump-shouldered, woebegone, but Shaughnessy was militarily erect and trim and, at 6 feet and 190 pounds, as big as many of them.

"Boys," he began, "I am not to be addressed as 'Clark' or, especially, 'Soup.' To you, I am 'Mr. Shaughnessy' or 'Coach.' Nothing else. Now, I have a formation for you that if you learn it well, will take you to the Rose Bowl."

He stepped to the blackboard and sketched out an unusual alignment. The line he depicted was balanced. The quarterback was directly behind the center, actually touching him, and the remaining three backs were in a line behind him. Together, the backs formed the letter T. Shaughnessy began to diagram plays. "If you learn this play well, you will score five touchdowns with it this season," he said, the chalk hurrying across the board. Albert was skeptical but fascinated. "Five touchdowns on one play!" he said to himself. "We hardly scored five touchdowns all of last season."

Among Shaughnessy's more conspicuous talents was a knack for fitting the man to the position. Chuck Taylor had been a blocking back in the Warner system; Shaughnessy made him a guard in the T, a position at which he eventually made All-America. Vic Lindskog, a transfer from Santa Ana Junior College, also came to Stanford as a blocking back; Shaughnessy made him a center, and there he would prosper in professional football.

Shaughnessy was to describe the backfield he inherited as tailor-made for the T. The fullback, Norm Standlee, was a giant for his day at about 220 pounds, but he had the speed to run the ends, a skill never exploited in the single and double wings, but a requirement in the T. On quick openers from the new formation, Standlee would also hit the line at close to full speed, the impact carrying him for certain yardage. As a professional with the Bears and the San Francisco 49ers, he would be considered the quintessential fullback.

Pete Kmetovic had been a tailback in 1939, but he played sporadically because he could not pass well. He became Shaughnessy's left halfback, a remarkably shifty runner who, as the man most frequently in motion, became a superb pass receiver, a heretofore unplumbed talent. Hugh Gallarneau's abilities as a runner and receiver had been wasted in his previous duties as a wingback in the Warner formation. As right half in the T, a 190-pounder with speed and power, he was the perfect complement to Standlee and Kmetovic.

Shaughnessy hired Bernie Masterson, the Chicago Bears' quarterback of the previous season, to coach Albert in the intricacies of ball handling from under the center. In an astonishingly short time, the pupil became the master. Shaughnessy had known from the beginning that Albert would be his quarterback.

"Long before I went to Stanford I had heard of him," Shaughnessy wrote in *Football in War and Peace*, a book published in 1943. "I knew he fitted exactly the requirements of the T-Formation. Frankie, for example, was not used in [my] system as a blocker or a ball-carrier, assignments in which he would have been at a great disadvantage because he was neither strong nor fast. His talents were primarily those of a faker; he could fool people, and by temperament he ate up that sort of assignment. His talents were more intellectual and psychological than physical. He was a poker player if ever there was one, and the T-Formation gave him exactly the best opportunities to exploit those strengths of his to the utmost, at the same time covering up the shortcomings he had that would have put him at a great disadvantage in other styles of play."

Shaughnessy and Albert were opposites, the former solemn and pious, the latter puckish and irreverent, but opposites attracted to each other. Albert was the only Stanford player who dared trifle with the coach. For the amusement of his teammates, he would feign injury in practice, only to spring to life as Shaughnessy, grayfaced, approached on the run. Shaughnessy broke with many associates in his later life, but praised Albert, both as a player and a person, to his final days. Though he would later coach Norm Van Brocklin and Bob Waterfield, Albert remained, for him, "the greatest quarterback I've ever seen." And Albert, to the present, speaks reverently of Shaughnessy's "genius."

★　★　★

During the 30 days of spring practice and the intense preparations of September, Shaughnessy worked himself, his assistants and his players as few college teams have ever been worked. If the T were to fail, it would not be through lack of preparation. One evening, Stanford Athletic Director Al Masters complained angrily to the maintenance department that some idiot had left the lights on at the football practice field. The "idiot," he was advised, was Shaughnessy, and the lights were on because the team was still practicing.

Shaughnessy was never happier. "I've had 60 big kids, tough, rugged fellows who love football, coming out every day for a month, coming from classes and laboratories on the run just to practice, then running back after practice to wait on tables and the like. There's tremendous football spirit at Stanford."

But there were setbacks. In a scrimmage against the freshmen in the fall, the varsity was able to score only a single touchdown. Shaughnessy subsequently designed a single wing offense to be installed if the T should not work, although he did not tell the players, fearful of further eroding their confidence.

Newspaper accounts of the unusual goings-on at Palo Alto only occasionally referred to the new system as the T formation, reporters preferring to call it "The Shaughnessy System" or "Shaughnessy's new razzle-dazzle attack." One who did call it by its correct name was Bill Leiser of the San Francisco *Chronicle*. "No one knows for sure what kind of football the Indians will play from this new T-Formation," he wrote. "They start from the Notre Dame T and then stop looking like Notre Dame because they don't shift at all and never do get into the famous box formation. The man-in-motion may stop anywhere on the field. He changes the formation. Albert parks himself right behind the center and takes the ball directly from his hands on nearly all plays. It's football unlike any previously played on the Coast."

Stanford's opening game, with the University of San Francisco on Sept. 28, 1940, was to be the second in an unprecedented major-college doubleheader at San Francisco's Kezar Stadium. The first game matched Santa Clara with Utah. Across the Bay that day, the

California Golden Bears had a date with Michigan and its All-America tailback, Tommy Harmon, in a game considered much more significant than either of those at Kezar.

On the eve of the game, Shaughnessy delighted reporters covering his practice by dressing his team in their brilliant new game uniforms—bright cardinal jerseys and stockings, white helmets and pants—instead of in the sweat clothes ordinarily worn on the last practice of the week. It was a pity, the newsmen commented, that such fashionable raiment would be ripped to tatters by the street kids from San Francisco.

Santa Clara defeated Utah 34-13 in the opening game before a crowd of 34,000. Stanford and USF took the field shortly after 3:30 for the second game. Mac Speedie of Utah, later an All-Pro receiver with the Cleveland Browns, was showering in the Kezar locker room when the second game started. Disappointed in his team's defeat, he had no interest in watching another football game that day, so he lingered in the solitude of the dressing chamber. As he toweled off, a teammate burst through the door. "Hey," he shouted, "you got to see this to believe it. They've got the damnedest formation out there I've ever seen. You can't even follow the ball."

This historic game began rather sloppily. Because of penalties and fumbles, Stanford did not move the ball in its first two possessions, further evidence, skeptics agreed, that Shaughnessy's system was more baffling to those using it than to those it was being used against. The third time the Indians had the ball, however, the pieces began to fit. Albert passed 17 yards to Gallarneau, a play made easier because the USF secondary, transfixed by Albert's fake, failed to cover the receiver as he drifted in motion. Then Standlee burst through an immense hole for 20 more yards. Albert could not contain himself as he rushed into the huddle this time. "Hey," he shouted, "this stuff really works." Kmetovic scored the first touchdown of the game on a quick opener up the middle. He was not touched. It is entirely possible he was not even seen.

"You could tell by the holes we had that somebody was confused," says Kmetovic, now the Stanford rugby coach. "We were running right by people who didn't know we had the ball."

Defenses of that time were accustomed to seeing the ball centered some four or five yards to a tailback or a fullback. The essential problem then was to break down the massed blocking in front of the runner. Considering the inexperience of Stanford's line, that did not seem to be a problem. But somehow those linemen were almost as elusive as the backs; instead of standing there as if screwed into the ground, they seemed to come at the opposition from every direction but straight ahead.

Stanford's new offensive plays developed so quickly that being small in the line was not such a disadvantage. Defenders did not have to be held off for three or four seconds, as was the case in the single wing. The T formation required only "brush blocking," a technique wherein the defender was merely neutralized for a moment or two. Even more confusing, however, was what was going on behind the line of scrimmage. Deception, in those days, was most often represented by a fullback spinning and handing off to another back or by the tailback reversing the ball to a wingback on a fake sweep. Then again, the fullback might hand the ball to the blocking back—the quarterback in the single wing—on a fake line plunge; the blocking back, in turn, might lateral the ball to the tailback or wingback—the buck-lateral series. Defenses were accustomed to such tactics and it was not often they were caught completely off guard.

★ ★ ★

But with the Stanford T, the defense never got a look at the ball to begin with. Albert, his hands cupped between the center's legs, received the ball, wheeled so that his back was to the line and faked the ball to one or two runners before either giving it off or keeping it himself. On the quick openers, he simply turned to hand the ball to a back running at almost full speed into the line. The man-in-motion was a further dilemma to the defense. From the straight-T alignment, one of the backs would leave his position before the center snap and move laterally along the line, hurrying downfield with the snap as either a pass receiver or a decoy. Secondary defenses had never dealt with such a caper before.

All of Stanford's plays required timing that seemed beyond the capabilities of college players. Even the Chicago Bears, for all of their experience with the system, had had only sporadic success up to that time and, significantly, none of the other pro teams had seen fit to emulate them. But Shaughnessy had the right people. And Lord knows, they had worked at the task. The timing, even in the T's debut, was exquisite.

"They kept changing guards on me," Taylor says. "They couldn't handle the quick openers, didn't even seem to recognize them.

Obviously, their linemen had instructions to get lower and lower. Eventually, they got so low, all I had to do was fall on my man."

Stanford won 27-0, outgaining USF 247 net yards to eight. The score would have been higher had Shaughnessy not used 42 players in the game, and this in the years before free substitution. Still, the importance of the game did not immediately sink in. Harmon's spectacular performance against Cal—he scored four touchdowns, three on runs of more than 50 yards—upstaged the show at Kezar. Harmon alone would have been enough to command the headlines, but he had unexpected help from a spectator, one H. J. (Bud) Brennan, who, in his frustration, leaped from his seat during one Harmon jaunt and attempted to tackle him near the Cal goal line. Photographs of the balding and paunchy fan groping for the great halfback occupied full pages in all of the principal Bay Area newspapers the next day.

The introduction of the T had been overshadowed by events both sublime and ridiculous, but the full significance was not entirely lost. "This type of football is different," wrote Leiser. "Why, some of those Stanford kids running away from the play actually had defenders chasing them harder than other defenders were chasing the ballcarrier." George Malley, the USF coach—described in the *Chronicle* as looking like "a man who had just seen a ghost" —could only shake his head in disbelief after the game. "We were baffled, naturally, by all that running around in the backfield."

★ ★ ★

Spectators experienced as much difficulty locating the ball as did the bewildered USF defenders. As with most occasions of this sort, the number of people who claim to have been there must now exceed a million, but one who really was on hand was Lou Spadia, former president of the San Francisco 49ers. "No one was prepared for what we saw," he says. "I couldn't tell where the ball was. No one around me could."

The game made an instant star of Albert, and for deeds never before celebrated. His passing and kicking were properly applauded, but it was his mystifying ball handling that enchanted the public. He had added a new dimension to the game, created, in fact, a new vocabulary. "Ball handling?" What had that to do with football? "Hand-offs?" What were they? "Quick openers?" Faking with the ball is an essential of T quarterbacking, but when the formation was new it was a unique gift, and Albert was not merely good at it, he was a genius.

"Don't forget Frank did all this before anybody had done it," says Vucinich. "All that spinning, faking and handling the ball off quickly. Kids learn that stuff today in grammar school. Frank learned it all in one spring, and no one's ever been better at it. If we hadn't had an Albert, we probably wouldn't have used the T, and the game would be entirely different from what it is today."

After the USF game, Shaughnessy discarded his single wing playbook. In one day he had transformed the game's most popular formation into an anachronism.

★ ★ ★

"I don't think anybody really believed us until the seventh or eighth game," says Albert, turning the pages of a scrapbook entitled *Stanford*. He is trim and jaunty at 57, though the still-handsome Peck's Bad Boy face is lined with the years and scarred from too much football, and the once black hair is gray. He speaks crisply, as if still barking signals, but always with a trace of amusement. Frankie Albert has had mostly good times.

Though he does not dwell on the past, he happily relives it. He pulls out a copy of *Collier's*, which has him on the cover riding the shoulders of joyous coeds. The face in the picture betrays not a hint of embarassment.

Investments, including one with his old pro team, the 49ers, have made him a man of comparative means, with time to enjoy his family, his tennis and the company of old friends. He and his wife of 35 years, Marty, live in a lavishly appointed condominium scarcely a mile from the Stanford campus.

"We just kept winning," Albert says, looking with wonder at the succession of headlines heralding victory. "Shaughnessy was like a fortune-teller. He'd tell us this or that would work and it always did. He'd invent new plays in the middle of a game and, heck, no one had more plays than we already had. Hardly anybody has now. The guy was always thinking. We all respected him. Years later, I'd never smoke in his presence. He had that kind of power over us."

They were called the "Wow Boys," an invention of publicity men, the nickname derived from the "Vow Boys" as much as from the team's capacity to astonish. But not every win was as easy as the first that year. They were behind in several games, winning, as often as not, in the closing minutes with some act of trickery. Word of the new formation spread quickly through the coaching fraternity, and desperate measures were taken to cope with it. The coaches of two future opponents, Shaw of Santa Clara and Tex Oliver of Oregon, watched the USF game with mounting alarm from the Kezar press box. "I saw so much that I can't go to sleep now," said Oliver. "That stuff requires defense."

At a time when defenses tended to be static, Stanford faced 10 separate setups in 10 games, including the Rose Bowl. Among these was a 4-3, devised by Oregon State's Lon Stiner, that would become the standard pro football defense of the 1960s and '70s. The Wow Boys beat it 28-14.

Stanford's offense was so versatile that new stars emerged each week. Kmetovic or Gallarneau might win the day with long runs or pass receptions, or Standlee might dominate with his power thrusts. But Albert was the pilot of the machine and his daring and generalship kept every opponent off balance. And for all of his cerebral skills, he was a splendid athlete in the bargain. Against Oregon State he averaged 52.6 yards on eight punts. In the team's one poorly played game, his point-after-touchdown kick defeated stubborn Santa Clara 7-6. He called all the plays, did the punting and place-kicking, returned punts and was the team's best defensive back. He also added another play to the Stanford repertoire when, spotting a massed defense, he elected not to give the ball to Fullback Vucinich on a fourth-quarter play in a game against Washington, but kept it himself and ran alone away from the blocking flow for 14 yards. Vucinich, who had expected to receive the handoff, was as baffled by the maneuver as was Washington. It was Albert's first "bootleg," a device he would employ to great advantage with the 49ers.

★   ★   ★

In the Rose Bowl game, Nebraska scored the first time it had the ball. Albert trotted over to Shaughnessy, who was staring gloomily and said, "Don't worry, Coach, we haven't had the ball yet." Stanford won 21-13, Gallarneau scoring twice, on an 11-yard run and a 40-yard pass from Albert, and Kmetovic on a 39-yard punt return. Stanford gained a total of 347 yards to Nebraska's 128. The T had established itself against a tough intersectional opponent that had had a month to prepare for it.

Albert was virtually a unanimous All-America selection for 1940, and Shaughnessy was named Coach of the Year.

Three weeks before the Rose Bowl, the Chicago Bears scored an astonishing 73-0 win over the Washington Redskins in the NFL championship game. Shaughnessy, whose association with Halas dated to 1933, had taken time out from his own team's preparations to assist his old collaborator before the title game. Halas had described Shaughnessy as "the greatest play designer in the game," and the Bears' offense was at least partly his creation. In Sid Luckman, Halas also had found the quarterback he required to make the T work as it was meant to. What had once been an offense rooted to the brute power of Fullback Bronko Nagurski had become a magic show. The electrifying successes, one after the other, of the two T teams incited a revolution in both college and professional football. It was as if the two teams had had the same coaching staffs, which, in a way, they had. Shaughnessy watched Halas' landmark victory and Halas watched Shaughnessy's. They shared a common sense of vindication.

After graduating from Stanford in 1942 and serving three years in the Navy during World War II, Albert, still a legend, signed to play with the 49ers in their first season, 1946. A pioneer once again, he was the box-office draw the team required for survival in the new All-America Conference. His passing, bootlegging, quick kicking and incurable gambling endeared him to a postwar generation of fans hungry for entertainment. Albert was flashy; he was also very good. In 1948 he threw 29 touchdown passes to eclipse a pro football record held by Luckman. He also scored eight times to help account for an amazing 37 touchdowns. He was the team's quarterback when it entered the NFL in 1950.

Albert retired after the 1952 season. In his last game, a win over the Green Bay Packers, he flamboyantly tore off his helmet, jersey, socks and shoes and tossed them to admiring youngsters on the Kezar playing field. He coached the 49ers for three years, 1956 through '58, and nearly won a championship, his '57 team losing 31-27 to the Detroit Lions in a heartbreaking playoff for the Western Conference championship, after leading 24-7 at the half. Disillusioned, Albert quit coaching after 1958, declaring himself "emotionally unsuited" to the task. To those who questioned his decision, he replied, as he still does, "Have you ever seen a happy coach?" Albert would never again risk that sort of unhappiness, preferring to dabble in a variety of business ventures—real estate, restaurants, automobiles—most of which earned him healthy profits.

His old teammates seem surprised that he is not even more successful, that he is not the chairman of some conglomerate or the president of a television network, so unwavering is their faith in his originality and resourcefulness. But Albert has stayed out of the big races. "I'm not too much for working," he says. "I've got everything in life I require. I've just been lucky."

Shaughnessy quit Stanford after the 1941 season when it became apparent the university would discontinue football during World War II. He moved first to the University of Maryland, then to Pittsburgh and back to Maryland again. In 1948 he became the head coach of the Los Angeles Rams, a job he held for only two seasons before owner Dan Reeves—charging Shaughnessy with creating "internal friction"—replaced him with Joe Stydahar. Shaughnessy's own parting remarks were characteristic: "When Stydahar gets through with the Rams, I can take any high school team in the country and beat him." It was hardly a prophecy; the Rams won a division championship in Stydahar's first season and shattered almost every league record for passing yardage and scoring.

Except for a fill-in job at the University of Hawaii in 1965, Shaughnessy never worked again as a head coach. He served Halas as an assistant from 1951 to 1962. When he quit, he complained of "differences," even with so rare a friend.

Clark Shaughnessy died on May 15, 1970 in Santa Monica, Calif. at the age of 78, his reputation for genius somehow intact despite a 149-116-17 record that scarcely compared with those of similarly acclaimed coaches. It was a reputation constructed largely on one all-triumphant, incandescent season. Never after 1940 did he find the right combination of time, circumstances and people to serve his restless intellect and turbulent energies. But it can be said that, perhaps more than any coach in the game's history, he left an enduring heritage.

There were many mourners at Shaughnessy's funeral, but the largest representation by far came from the Wow Boys of 1940. To them, prominent men in business and the professions, he remains "Mr. Shaughnessy, Coach."

Andy's Eulogy Still Lives

Good Lord, the Andy Smith Eulogy lives!

Indeed, there it is listed right below the Powderpuff football team reception on Cal's Big Game Week press handout—"Big Game Bonfire Rally, 8 to 9 p.m., Hearst Greek Theater. Featured will be Professor Garff Wilson delivering the 'Andy Smith Eulogy.'"

Well, if it's true the times, they are a-changin', at this pace we needn't mark Armageddon on next month's calendar.

Garff Wilson, now a professor of rhetoric and dramatic art at Cal, as well as assistant to the chancellor in charge of protocol, is both the author of the eulogy and, for the past 20 years at least, its reader. Among the U.C. people of the past quarter century, he is as identified with it as Judy Garland once was with "Over the Rainbow."

The beginning was 1948.

★ ★ ★

"I had been watching the Big Game parade," recalls Wilson, then only a professor of speech, "when I heard my name being paged from the sound truck. It was like hearing the voice of Jehovah. What had happened was that after two years of reading something on coach Andy Smith, radio announcer Mel Venter had refused to do it at the rally that year. They wanted me to write a substitute.

"But I protested I didn't know Andy Smith, that he had died long before I entered the university. The Rally Committee told me not to worry. They had all the clips on him. So I locked myself in my office with a sandwich and a cup of coffee, and I wrote it in about two and a half hours. Bud Hobbs, a student, read it that year and the next.

"Bud graduated in 1950 and so that year, somebody from the Rally Committee phoned me and asked if I knew where he could find a copy of the Eulogy. I said that since I wrote it, I had the only one. They asked me to read it, and that's it."

★ ★ ★

144

*Andy Smith was coach of the so-called California Wonder
Teams of the early 1920s, which didn't lose a game in five years.*

*He was considered a great innovator in his time. He was also,
despite a remarkably homely face, a man of considerable charm
and conviviality. His wife, who divorced him, claimed he spent so
much time at the Elks Club celebrating his great victories, she never
saw him.*

*He was also an incurable sentimentalist who could say, "We do
not want men who will lie down bravely to die, but men who will
fight valiantly to live. . . ."*

*In his will, he requested his ashes be strewn over the Stadium, a
wish that was duly respected after his death in January of 1926.
Fifteen thousand mourners stood outside the stadium at his funeral
as an airplane sprinkled the ashes.*

★   ★   ★

This scene provides the punch-line for Wilson's eulogy:

*". . . the multitudes stood silent while an airplane circled over-
head; then it dipped low; and as it passed over the locked and silent
stadium, it scattered the ashes of Andy Smith—as he had wished—
over the field where he had worked and fought his battles, there to
remain forever."*

*This is read by Wilson as the Cal Glee Club hums a medley of
school songs in the background. The audience stands holding can-
dles before a great log fire in the amphitheater. And when Wilson
finishes, a bugler in the hills plays taps. Then the head yell leader
quietly requests that everyone remain standing for the singing of
"All Hail."*

*Let me tell you, when I was in school, this was sure-fire. But
now?*

★   ★   ★

*"A tradition," says Wilson, "is like a living thing. It is born, it
matures and it dies. I'm not sure where this one is. But if some Big
Game night, I should notice that the crowd is laughing or inter-
rupting me, I have made up my mind to walk off the stage, saying
only, 'It's usefulness has ended.'*

"That and no more."

The Rooting Section:
A Distinct Subculture

A certain understandable confusion exists as to the origins of organized cheering or rooting, as in, say, "Oskee wa wa, Skini wa wa!" or "Oooooo Pig Souiee!" The Greeks, as we all by now know, were enthusiastic chanters. Indeed, the Greek chorus may have been the first rooting section in recorded history although a vision springs to mind of prehistoric man rooting himself on while in mortal combat with the creature of his day—"Hold that Lion!" "Three Cheers and a Sabre Tooth Tiger!"

But as far as we know, it was the Romans, perverting, as was their wont, most things Greek, who converted simple Demosthenes spell yells into military exhortations. The earliest yell leaders, in fact, were all military people, phalanx commanders and the like. The Romans overran the known world crying out, "Give me a C, give me an A, give me an E, give me an S-A-R!" The Mamelukes, those testy Egyptians warriors, scared the living bejeezus out of every foe up to and including Napoleon with their cacaphonous shrieks. The

Prussians were notoriously noisy, too, and it is they, it seems, who must assume responsibility for shouting out the first, "Hurrah!" or as subsequent generations have condensed it, "Rah, rah!" Even Hitler is said to have used as the inspiration for his Party rallies the American rooting section. "Sieg Heil!" was merely his chilling translation of "Give 'em the Axe!"

Both the Union and Confederate armies in this country's Civil War were rooted in rooting and many of their battle cries found their way into the sport which immediately succeeded the conflict—football. The Rebel Yell is still heard throughout the South on football Saturdays, although it was not the first of the war cheers to enter the rooter's lexicon. That distinction belongs to the so-called "Rocket Yell" of the Seventh Regiment of New York, Army of the Potomac. The Seventh had passed through Princeton, New Jersey, en route to combat and had much impressed the university's undergraduates with its spirit and ingenious songs and yells. A particular favorite was the soldiers' "Siss, boom, ah!" yell, which was merely an onomatopoetic account of the ignition, explosion and final extinction of an airborne rocket.

And so it was that "Siss, boom, ah!" or, as it has been shouted, "Siss boom, bah!" was heard from the Princeton side of the field at the first American football game between that distinguished institution and Rutgers in 1869. Princeton students later added certain touches of sophistication to this basically simple-minded shout, so that eventually it became the familiar, "Ray, ray, ray . . . Tiger, Tiger, Tiger . . . Siss, siss, siss . . . Boom, boom, boom . . . Aaaaaa aaaaah . . . Princeton! Princeton! Princeton!" A Confederate victory might have spared the Nation that one.

Yale's traditional "Brek-ek-ek-ex-koax" yell followed Princeton's by some 15 years, but it has much tonier breeding, reaching back, as it does, to classical drama. Signficantly, the yell was first delivered not as a motivation for a football team but as homage to a professor of classics, one Frank Bigelow Tarbell. The originators were members of "The Thirteen" eating club. One of their innovative number, The Rev. Chauncey W. Goodrich, was to reflect on the Tarbell yell some years later:

"In the spring of our sophomore year—that of 1884—prizes were won by two members of the club, and to celebrate this it was decided to hold a festive dinner at the restaurant to which college men then repaired for such purposes. We had all been studying with Professor Tarbell 'The Frogs' of Aristophanes and had been in-

trigued by the cadences of the frog chorus. As we sat, metamorphi-
cally speaking, over our 'wine and cigars,' it was proposed that we
shape the chorus into a cheer and give it that evening under the
windows of Professor Tarbell.

"A little later, after having rehearsed the cheer to the point of
perfection, we walked across the campus about 11 o'clock and,
standing by the western entry to Durfee, shouted the cheer full-
throated twice:

'Brek, ek-ek, ex.
Koax, koax.
Brek-ek, ek.
Koax, koax.
O-op, O-op.
Parabalou
Tarbell!"

Harvard, as might be expected, insists that its "Regular Cheer"
was truly the first to be heard in the land. The "Regular Cheer"—
three "Har . . . vards," followed by seven "rahs" and a "fight,
team, fight!"—is, however, scarcely in the same class with Aristophanes.

The University of Minnesota would surely not be so bold as to
contest the precursory credentials of "Siss, boom, ah!" "Brek-ek-
ek!" and "rah, rah, rah!" But it does insist on laying title to the first
cheerleader, a chap named Johnny Campbell, who was so overwhelmed by the events of a Golden Gopher contest in 1898 that he
could keep his seat no longer. Campbell leapt onto the field in front
of the grandstand and, capering maniacally, compelled his fellows
to join him in crying out, "Rah, rah, rah, Minnesota!" It was a
stirring moment and from then on, Minnesota was to have a yell
leader. Within the next decade, most other colleges with football
teams joined in.

It remained, however, for the West Coast to add necessary
theatrical touches to the rooting performance. In 1899, one year
after Campbell's historic leap, University of California rooters in
Berkeley formed a Block C in their section by wearing blue and
gold caps in the proper relationship. Nine years later, Cal rooters
introduced the first card stunts, static presentations that appeared
to spectators across the field as giant advertisements.

In 1922, USC added movement to the cards by spelling out
"Trojans" one letter at a time. And two years later, at Oregon State

College, the first animated card stunts were conceived by OSC rooters who flipped their cards in a pre-arranged pattern to show an Oregon State Beaver swatting a lemon yellow "O"—for Oregon—with his tail.

There have been some innovations since, but none of such enduring significance. In 1958, the Naval Academy introduced the "remote root," in which cheers from Midshipmen in the Academy field house were broadcast over loudspeakers placed behind the Navy bench in an away game with Boston University. Despite the physical absence of their rooters, the Navy players were sufficiently inspired by the electronic cheers to defeat B.U. 28-14.

There have also been several instances of, shall we say, Watergated rooting sections. This occurs when dirty tricks units from one school infiltrate the rooting section of another to render its card stunts inoperative. The ultimate achievement here must be credited to the California Institute of Technology pranksters who, in the Rose Bowl game of 1961, contrived to rewrite the University of Washington card stunt script so that when Washington students hoisted cards they assumed would spell out "Huskies," "Cal Tech" appeared instead.

And yet through all these years and all those stunts one rooting section seems somehow to stand apart, shall we say, from the mob. That would be the University of California's at Berkeley in the boisterous years immediately following World War II; rooters so singular they were celebrated on the cover of Life Magazine and castigated by puritans everywhere. Their fame, their infamy, actually was so great that, the football team aside, they became drawing cards themselves. While other rooting sections of the time hewed rather closely to pre-war standards, the Cal section cut its own bawdy course. There were some imitators, but none could truly capture the uniquely perverse spirit.

It was a peculiar time, a kind of mini-1920s, a dear dead time that I nonetheless recall so well, for as a teenage lower-classman, I was there. The war had ended and the veterans had returned, many to enter college under the G.I. Bill. There was one obvious difference between the male rooters then and now—they were older. And because they had only just returned from military service, they were, in the moments of free time they allowed themselves, recklessly hedonistic, hell bent on compensating for the years they had lost in military service.

Not that this set them apart from other returning G.I.s in other universities and colleges. What made the Cal section unusual was both its great size—10,000 or more on an average Saturday—and its all-male center section, numbering 5000 or more. The side sections were for women and men with dates. The middle was stag. And as it happened, these were men bursting with stored energy, spoiling, as it were, for action.

The all-male central rooting section had long been a Cal tradition —thousands of masculine voices raised in exhortation gave a certain dramatic flavor to the cheering. It was a tradition that in the decade after the war would be put to a terrible test.

This is not to say that the all-male rooters preceding the Forties were necessarily orderly. But they *were* younger, and because of the circumstances of their time, less free. The post-war rooters were unlike any before or after them. They were, for one, far more experienced as drinking men, grownups not willing to regard an evening in the company of a six-pack as a binge. They were also men who had been forced to grow up in a hurry. And they *were* older. The senior classes of the late Forties contained not a few men who were into their thirties. There was a true generation gap then between these comparatively grizzled oldtimers and the youngsters entering college from high school.

The older men had a profound influence on the youngsters, who became their devoted servants and their shameless emulators. On Saturdays, the kids were as prankish as their elders. The older men worked hard, the better to get through school and get cracking on careers long denied them, and they played even harder. The youngsters were not so industrious, but they were diligent hedonists. The weekend, even for the non-veterans seemed like a shore leave, a three-day pass.

On Saturdays, they stormed Memorial Stadium, fortified in varying dosages with "Jackie Jensen Orange Juice," a frozen-orange-juice-vodka concoction named in tribute to the ranking football hero of the time. And so by game-time, this "rooting section," this mass assemblage of not-so-young, not-entirely-sober men, was ready not so much for a game of football as for a riotous party.

Still, with football and college the rooters *were* capable of being inspired, angered. There was a smallish Polynesian—possibly a citizen of the Philippines—who, though no official yell leader, served in that capacity when the mood seized him. And when seized, he could drive the "Jackie Jensen Orange Juice" imbibers to a towering frenzy. He would generally appear shortly before kickoff, usually on demand. He was a plump, vibrant, mysterious figure who would address his constituents not from the yell leader's platform but from a position just behind the players' bench. He swayed there rhythmically, beginning his chant in a low, scarcely audible voice. "Heeya, heeya, heeya . . ." Gradually, he would increase the volume and the intensity until finally the entire men's rooting section would be caught up in his spell, shouting with him hysterically the mesmerizing "Heeya, heeya, heeya!" Ordinarily the chant culminated in an abrupt shout of "Drop Dead!" a popular if singularly uninspired expression of the time. Eventually, stronger language seemed more appropriate to this incantation.

The rooting section was deplored and rebuked everywhere.

Profanity would not be denied, however. It was the language of the serviceman. And soon the male rooters developed yells, independent of the appointed yell leaders, that were invariably in questionable taste. "Go Bears" was insufficient to the needs of men caught up in obscene inspiration. The rooters would count out the yardage—"one, two, three!"—as a hapless referee stepped off penalties against the home team, then at the finish of the march, question en masse the parentage of the offending official.

At the very beginning of this period, in 1946, the male rooters systematically dismembered their own seats after a disappointing loss to Stanford, a school that had abandoned football for the duration. But violence, other than verbal, was rare. These men had been swearing, yes, like sailors for maybe four years. They saw nothing unusual about doing it in a body. The cheers, if nothing else, had shock value.

Still, as the years passed and the rooting responsibility fell to the pupils of the veterans and then to the pupils of the pupils of the veterans, a certain disintegration took place. What had been original, even funny, if tasteless, became merely gross indulgence. Returning servicement could be forgiven their sins. Spoiled brats could never be forgiven theirs.

Finally, in October of 1959, the men's rooting section was disbanded by order of the Student Executive Committee on grounds of continuous "rowdiness and vulgarity." Football officials had testified that they would accept assignments "anywhere but Cal" because of the "vile language" directed at them from the rooting section. By executive fiat, women would now be permitted to sit in the center section. The stag show was over.

It seems a little sad now that the section should perish under judgment so harsh and unsparing. But with the changing times, the male rooters would never have survived in a body. Their own excess doomed them and their bibulous tradition is best left to memory. Still, for those of us who lived through it, distance has given that memory infinite charm.

Time and circumstance made these heeya-heeya shouters of long ago something rather special. It is safe to assume that as long as intercollegiate sports thrive, rooting sections will persist. But I rather firmly suspect we shall never see and hear another like the one that scourged Strawberry Canyon a quarter century ago. Maybe it is just as well.

This Is What It's All About

I think I speak for both coaches in Sunday's forthcoming first annual traditional regular season classic when I say we're in tough.

All year long we've been playing them one at a time, but after Sunday there's no tomorrow. It all comes down to this: we'll just have to come at them all the way. To win, we'll have to go out and get it.

Football is an emotional game. The team with desire generally wins. Of course, we'll both be up for this one. And we're both physical teams. A lot of our starters will be playing with pain, but you've got to pay the price in this game. That's the mark of a pro.

★ ★ ★

Both of us coaches have the greatest respect for our opponent. The Raiders have fine personnel, the 49ers have good football players. Gene Washington is an outstanding athlete, Fred Biletnikoff is an excellent receiver with good moves.

Both teams have good balance. The Raiders will establish their running game, then hurt you deep. John Brodie is a pure passer, and Daryle Lamonica can throw the bomb with anybody in the business. You always know you've been in a ballgame when you play the 49ers. They don't blitz a lot, but their front four, the down linemen, can get to the passer.

The Raider linebackers are extremely mobile, and their Tom Keating makes up in quickness what he lacks in size. The defensive backs play the bump and run as well as anyone. And that Dave Grayson—he goes to the ball.

We coaches won't have to tell our athletes much to get them high for this one. They're professionals, grown men. There's a lot at stake here, and you can forget about the odds in a game like this. Both teams will be giving 100 per cent. That's what it takes.

★ ★ ★

153

The team that makes the fewest mistakes will probably win. Those turnovers will kill you. They're the difference between winning and losing.

We coaches plan to make certain adjustments—offensively and defensively. The Raiders will sometimes come at you with an odd line, which confuses the blocking assignments and will shut off your running game, which you've got to establish. Offensively, they'll give you a brown formation and blunt to the weak side.

The 49ers, as I've said, are a very physical team. Their Ken Willard is the best in the game running inside the tackles. He's very strong, a good blocker, and he has great hands. You don't have to tell anybody about John Brodie. He's right up there with the best. Always has been. He can hurt you.

★　★　★

The biggest improvement in the 49ers this year has been in their special teams, the suicide squads, the gizzards. They provide excellent coverage on both punts and kickoffs, and their Bruce Taylor is a fine return man. He's got good hands and quick feet.

Their Bruce Gossett is always a threat inside the 40. He's one of the best medium-to-long kickers in the game.

And what can you say about George Blanda, the old man? He's a money ballplayer, a pressure performer. Most men his age are content to watch the game on television. Not George, the old man. He's a real competitor, a handy guy to have around. His record speaks for itself.

In a game like this, past performances don't mean a thing. This one, like all others, will be won down in the Pit, where the big linemen will play matchup. What happens there in that hand-to-hand combat will determine the outcome.

★　★　★

We coaches never underestimate any opponent. On a given day, any team can beat you. You've got to be up for every game, take it to 'em. The team that wants it most will get it. That's what it's all about. It's the name of the game. Welcome to the National Football League.

I hope I've made myself perfectly clear.

The Battle is Rejoined

With the Giants contending again, the old San Francisco-Los Angeles rivalry has been rekindled, as have memories of Dodger-Giant feuds past

A Los Angeles Dodger *catcher* once threw a brushback ball at a San Francisco Giant *pitcher*, whereupon the pitcher conked the catcher with a baseball bat. A Giant manager and a Dodger coach got into a fistfight right in the middle of batting practice one day. When a scorer from a Los Angeles newspaper robbed a Giant pitcher of a no-hitter, a San Francisco newspaper denounced the larcenous act in an editorial. A Giant manager once had the Candlestick Park groundkeeper muddy up the base paths to bog down a Dodger base stealer. An umpire refused to allow a Giant batter to take first base, even though he had been hit with a pitch. There was a time when the Dodgers and the Giants attracted 700,000 to 800,000 fans a year for their games against one another

in Los Angeles and San Francisco. And on a fine October afternoon, champagne flowed through the streets of San Francisco.

Ah, but that was long ago. And what had been the game's most
torrid rivalry has become tepid, has it not? Then why did Giant
Pitcher John Montefusco say of the Dodgers only a week ago, "A
lot of us can't stand those guys. They just get under our skin." And
why will some 200,000 fans watch the teams play four games in
Candlestick Park this week? No, the bitter old feud is not dead.
Sure, it lay dormant for a while, but the resurgence of the Giants
this season has revived it, and if the spectator response is any indi-
cation—and it certainly is—the rivalry has never been livelier.

In May, when the two teams last met, 153,113 fans saw three
games in Los Angeles and 145,614 watched three more in San Francisco, the crowd of 56,103 on May 28 establishing a record for the
Giants in San Francisco. There will soon be ample opportunity for
more records because the Giants and Dodgers play eight times in an
11-day span beginning this weekend. This stretch could well settle
the hash of one or the other in the National League West, where
upstart San Francisco has held a narrow lead over the expected
divisional contenders, Los Angeles and Cincinnati, for most of the
season. As a result, the Giants figure to draw more than half as
many fans in the nine home games with the Dodgers this year as
they did for all their games at Candlestick in 1977. San Francisco's
home attendance is more than double what it was at this time a
season ago, and it already exceeds last year's total of 700,056 by
more than 300,000. Clearly, Giant baseball is all the rage in
the Bay Area again. In saloons and restaurants, on the floors of the
brokerage houses, in the North Beach coffeehouses, in the parks
and on the Bay, the most pressing question these days is "What's
the score?"

There are hidebound traditionalists who still contend that the
true Dodger-Giant rivalry died when the teams moved west in
1958. They would be right only with regard to their first year in
California, when San Franciscans and Angelenos felt a rare kin-
ship, both being major league rookies. The chumminess could not
last, however, because the physical and spiritual differences
between the two cities are recognized even by those who understand neither. Isn't Los Angeles the place where everyone wears
sunglasses? And, oh yes, isn't San Francisco the town Anita Bryant
wouldn't be caught dead in? Both, in fact, are exceedingly complex
communities. Los Angeles is a good deal more than Beverly Hills;

much of it and its myriad suburbs are inhabited by politically and socially conservative Middle Americans. San Francisco is not just another pretty face. It is a tough town with a healthy sense of its own identity. One city is spreading, forever reaching beyond its borders; the other is compact, inward-turned. You confuse them at your peril. The rivalry between the cities, San Francisco Chronicle columnist Herb Caen once wrote, "is a reflex built in at birth. It is firmly a part of the mystique of each city, and why not? It's fun to have an object of automatic disdain so close at hand."

The transplanted ballplayers of the late '50s soon absorbed this sense of merry enmity, and a succession of unusual occurrences helped give Giants vs. Dodgers, in its California incarnation, a character quite distinct from New York vs. Brooklyn. The first such incident demonstrated that even a scorer's decision can exacerbate municipal prejudices. In 1959, Sam Jones, a laconic right-hander who gnawed a toothpick while he pitched, was the ace of the Giants' staff. On the night of June 30, in the Los Angeles Coliseum, he had a no-hitter working in the eighth inning when Jim Gilliam of the Dodgers hit an easy bouncer to the infamously maladroit Giant shortstop, Andre Rodgers. True to form, Rodgers bobbled the ball, picked it up and, aware that further effort would only compound his folly, made no throw to first. The official scorer, Charlie Park of the Los Angeles Mirror-News, did not hesitate in calling Gilliam's grounder a base hit. Jones nearly swallowed his toothpick. Members of the San Francisco press shouted imprecations, but Park resolutely rejected all appeals. Base hit! Russ Hodges, broadcasting the game home to San Francisco, was tremulous with rage. "If ever a man deserved a no-hit game, Sam Jones did tonight," he bellowed into the KSFO microphone. "The ball was a routine grounder."

The controversy did not die that night. The Chronicle, a wag of a newspaper, seized the opportunity to portray Park's decision as the embodiment of the Southern California mentality and to show up Charlie as the sort of bounder who would willingly rob the North of its drinking water and its no-hitters. There are, the Chronicle editorialized, "dark and secret things, unrelated to reality and governed by no law of man or nature, that happen all the time in the Los Angeles Coliseum. . . . Whatever the explanation, the facts are intolerable to San Franciscans who regard baseball as a sane pastime, bound by logical rules, fairly imposed. They don't like to have indignities inflicted on Sam Jones' no-hitter. This is a matter of principle, not sectionalism—a moral consideration which holds that it will be a cold day in Candlestick Park when any Dodger pitcher gets closer to an official no-hitter than the Jones boy did in the Los Angeles Coliseum."

The editorial writer had no way of knowing just how many cold days there would be in Candlestick Park, because the new stadium was still under construction in 1959, a matter of no small moment then. The Giants were playing in 23,000-seat Seals Stadium in a year in which, to their considerable surprise, they found themselves pennant contenders. In late September they were leading the league by two games and facing the prospect of playing the city's first World Series in a minor league park. The Dodgers resolved this dilemma by sweeping a three-game series in San Francisco, taking the lead themselves and pressing on to whip the White Sox and become California's first world champions. The battle now was truly joined.

The Giants avenged this humiliation three years later by tying the Dodgers on the last day of the season after L.A. had led by four with only seven games to play. The Dodgers' collapse was just as complete as the Giants' had been in '59; they lost six of those final games, the last two defeats coming by shutouts. In the subsequent playoff for the pennant, the Giants won two of three, thereby earning the privilege of losing to the Yankees in the World Series. It was a season in which Giant Manager Alvin (Swamp Fox) Dark had groundkeeper Matty Schwab drench the base paths, purportedly to keep loose dirt from blowing in the wind, but actually to keep Maury Wills of the Dodgers, who was en route to a record 104 steals, from blowing the Giants out of contention. The conspiracy was not lost on Los Angeles observers. One more squirt from Schwab's hose, wrote the L.A. *Times'* Jim Murray, "And the Red Cross would have declared second base a disaster area." Significantly, Schwab was voted a full $7,290 World Series share.

The 1962 race solidified the Dodgers' and Giants' new identities. Both teams had been reconstructed on the Pacific Coast, so there were few survivors from the New York-Brooklyn days. Sandy Koufax had never been a star in the East; he became one in Los Angeles. Wills and Tommy Davis, the new batting champion, had not even played in Brooklyn. Of the Giant stars, only Willie Mays retained a Coogan's Bluff patina. The others—Orlando Cepeda, Willie McCovey, Juan Marichal, Jimmy Davenport—all began their careers in San Francisco.

The summer of '62 saw the emergence of yet another new star—
the transistor radio. Because of the sunglasses, Nathanael West had
called Los Angeles "The City of the Blind"; with transistors now
affixed to Southern ears, it looked more like "The City of the Deaf."
And Bay Area fans were hardly less devoted to their tiny portable
radios. The War Memorial Opera House in San Francisco banned
the infernal machines after more than one diva complained of
applause and cheers curiously unrelated to the aria in progress.
Radios were not proscribed in Kezar Stadium, and on the last day
of the baseball season, John Brodie, quarterbacking the 49ers
against the Vikings, humbly raised his arms to still the deafening
cheer that had interrupted his signal-calling. Brodie was flattered
by the attention his modest efforts were receiving, until he
discovered the cheers were for the eighth-inning home run the
Cardinals' Gene Oliver had hit to beat the Dodgers and drop them
into a tie with the Giants.

The next Wednesday, the intermission at the matinee of the
musical *Oliver!* at San Francisco's Curran Theater was extended 25
minutes so that the theatergoers—and the actors—might hear the
final inning of the last playoff game on their radios. Bartenders
served customers only between innings. One downtown saloon had
five television sets going simultaneously, and lunch hour for many
that famous day dragged on into evening. When the Giants won, a
pandemonium not experienced in San Francisco since V-J Day
broke loose. At Grace Cathedral on Nob Hill, verger Charles
Agnews rushed to his carillon and played the *Hallelujah* chorus
from Handel's *Messiah*. Downtown traffic was jammed up until
after midnight, and an estimated 75,000 fans congregated at the airport to hail the conquerors on their return from Los Angeles. The
mob scene forced postponement of scheduled flights throughout
the evening.

James Meredith's historic enrollment at the University of Mississippi that week resulted in rioting in Oxford, Miss. and astronaut
Wally Schirra completed six orbits of the earth, but the *Chronicle's*
page-one headline the morning of Oct. 4 read, THE CITY FLIPS. As a
San Franciscan, Governor Pat Brown was not immune to the baseball hysteria. His campaign for reelection that year, he announced,
was the World Series of politics' and his opponent, one Richard
Nixon, was "one of the most controversial players in the game of
politics." Hardball politics, that is.

San Francisco's standing as the cultural capital of the West suffered mightily from the emotional response to the Giants' victory. "Good God," a woman told *The New Yorker's* Roger Angell, "people will think we're like Milwaukee or something."

The Giants and Dodgers were in another close race on Sunday, Aug. 22, 1965, when pitcher Juan Marichal came to bat leading off the third inning against Koufax. There had been bad feeling between the teams all year, which had manifested itself in a succession of beanball episodes. And the tenseness of their rivalry had been increased the previous Friday night, when Wills cajoled a catcher's-interference call out of the plate umpire, despite the insistence of Giant Catcher Tom Haller that Wills had deliberately touched his mitt with the bat. When San Francisco's Matty Alou tried the same gambit later in the game, interference was not called. The teams were seething that Sunday at Candlestick; Marichal had brushed back Wills in the second inning and Ron Fairly in the third.

Koufax' first pitch to Marichal was a called strike. The second was low and inside. In returning the ball to his pitcher, Dodger Catcher John Roseboro, no Marichal fan, threw hard and close to the pitcher's head. Marichal had half expected to be dusted off by the pitcher, but certainly not by the catcher. When he asked Roseboro what he was up to, the big catcher advanced on him menacingly. Marichal quickly recognized an unpromising situation: he was about to be set upon by a larger man wearing protective armor. Instinctively, he lashed out with the bat, fetching Roseboro a blow on the left side of the head. Players from both dugouts rushed onto the field, and Marichal was soon buried under a tangle of bodies. Beneath him was Plate Umpire Shag Crawford. Police finally quelled the disturbance on the diamond and prevented a near riot among the 42,807 fans.

Roseboro, bleeding from a two-inch wound, was led off the field by Dodger Trainer Wayne Anderson, and Crawford, upon regaining his feet and his dignity, tossed Marichal out of the game. After a 14-minute delay, the inning resumed, with Mays hitting a two-out, three-run homer off an obviously rattled Koufax. Those runs stood up, and the Giants moved to within a percentage point of the first-place Dodgers.

National League President Warren Giles fined Marichal a record $1,750 the next day and suspended him for eight playing dates. The Los Angeles press found the penalty insufficient to the crime. "Let a common citizen whack someone over the head with a bat and see what he gets," wrote the *Los Angeles Times'* Paul Zimmerman.

"This was baseball's chance to prove that attempted murder will not be condoned in the major leagues, and baseball blew it," the *Los Angeles Examiner* sermonized. "There is absolutely no justification, not even in the heat of a pennant race, for one man to attack another with a weapon on the playing field," said Roseboro reasonably, as he filed a $110,000 damage suit against Marichal and the Giants. The case was settled out of court 4½ years later, with Marichal paying Roseboro $7,500.

There was concern among Giant fans and assorted experts that Marichal, a sensitive man, might grow so disturbed over the ugly incident that his pitching would suffer. Hardly. In 1966, he had a 25-6 record. And in a final irony, he concluded his brilliant career in 1975 as a Dodger.

★ ★ ★

On May 31, 1968, in Dodger Stadium, Giant Catcher Dick Dietz was struck by a pitch thrown by Don Drysdale. It was the ninth inning, the bases were loaded, the count was 2-2, there was no one out and the Dodgers were leading 3-0. Dietz started toward first in the mistaken belief that he had broken up a shutout. But Plate Umpire Harry Wendelstedt ruled Dietz had not made a reasonable effort to avoid being hit by the ball. The pitch that hit him, became, therefore, ball three. The Giants' frantic protests were ignored, Manager Herman Franks was ejected, and Dietz was instructed to stand in again against Drysdale. He popped out to short left, and Drysdale retired the next two hitters to preserve his shutout.

An important shutout it was, because with it Drysdale tied a 64-year-old major league record of five consecutive scoreless games. In his next start. Drysdale threw yet another shutout to break the record. It was a considerable achievement, but it would not have been possible without Wendelstedt's unusual call on Dietz. "It was a gutsy call," said Drysdale's catcher, Jeff Torborg. "It would have been gutsy," responded Giant Vice-President Chub Feeney, "if he had made it in San Francisco."

The '60s were a fighting time, but soon after winning their divisional title in '71, the Giants faded from contention and the bitterness between the teams from San Francisco and Los Angeles subsided. Oh, in '73 there was a lively punch-up behind the batting cage between Giant Manager Charlie Fox and a Dodger coach named Lasorda, but it seemed merely an isolated incident between two middle-aged boys with long memories.

And yet it is a gentler moment that is frozen in memory. One thinks of Sam Cohen, the affable curmudgeon who operated the old Sam's Lane Club on San Francisco's chic Maiden Lane in the glory days of 1962. Sam proudly held a single share of stock in the Giants, and he made much of this minuscule investment, publishing a "minority report," which held the entire organization, from Matty Schwab to Horace Stoneham, to account. Publicly, Sam reviled the Giants; privately, he adored them. And on the day they won the pennant, his normally dour countenance was suffused with a roseate glow.

His bar erupted in cheers and backslapping as Lee Walls' final out settled into Willie Mays' basket catch on the television screen. Sam silently detached himself from the hullabaloo and retreated to the refrigerator, from which he withdrew a bottle of Paul Masson champagne. With scarcely a word, he passed through the revelers and out onto Maiden Lane. There, with an appropriate flourish, he popped the cork and emptied the contents onto the street. It was an act so prodigal that even the most hysterical celebrant paused to watch. Why was this old man pouring good California champagne into the street when he should be drinking it or, as in the locker-room ritual, dumping it on someone's head?

Sam never dignified the resultant inquiries with a response, but it now seems perfectly obvious why he did it. He loved his Giants and he loved his city, and at a time when both were at their best, it seemed right that champagne should flow through the streets. As anyone who was around then can tell you, it was a very San Francisco thing to do.

Great Big Fast Scout Report

Now that the barn door is, as they say, shut, it's time for us coaches to consider the upcoming football draft.

Naturally, we will be looking for the best athletes available, certainly not the worst. And we'll be after speed. If a man has speed, he can do a lot of things. Like run fast. We'll want size, too. You need that on a football team, particularly in the line and on the coaching staff.

Anyway, that's what we're basically hoping to draft—great big fast athletes. I can't speak for the other coaches, of course. Some of them may be looking for uncoordinated little slow guys, the 49er halfback type, as we call them in the game. But our scouts tell us that a big fast guy is better than a slow little guy on any given day. And those people know what they're talking about. They've spent all season traveling across this great land of ours watching college games and trying to score with airline stewardesses.

★ ★ ★

When we do get a chance to talk to them, our scouts tell us there are a number of fine prospects in the college ranks this year, many of whom are playing out of position. There are, for example, at least a half-dozen black quarterbacks we will naturally shift to wide receiver or defensive back. And there are a number of Polish fullbacks we think of as linebackers.

The thing is, if a guy is big and fast and a great athlete, he can play anywhere—except, of course, if he's black, quarterback.

★ ★ ★

I've been going over our scouting reports this morning. It's quite a change from looking at game films, most of which are dull and unimaginative when compared with Danish movies. Now, you will recall that we traded our third round draft pick for 1971 to Boston for its second round pick in 1972 who, in turn, traded our pick to

Cleveland for a shovel. That, as I figure it, gives us Green Bay's third, fourth and 16th pick. And, as a result of our 1964 trading, we have Baltimore's 7th pick, a black guy who is now playing wide receiver and defensive cornerback for New Orleans.

There are a number of people who go quickly in the first round, like Bob Foster and Jerry Quarry. So we'll have to come out smoking at the bell. White Owls are always nice that time of day. Let me review for you some of the fellows who will go quickly, probably before we ever get to them.

CHESTER RAYMOND: A wide receiver at Slippery Rock we'd shift to center. Great speed. Runs the 40 in 4.6 in his undershorts and bedroom slippers. Adequate upper body strength and pretty legs. Good driver for a Chinese.

MARSHALL THURGOOD: Won 72 varsity letters at Georgia State Teachers. Three of those were from a blonde in North Platte, Neb. Accumulated 12,000 yards rushing on fraternity week. Could be a fine running back or pulling guard. We see him as a kicking specialist.

WARREN (NASTY) HARDING: His age, 43, is a handicap. That and a perforated right arm. We like his speed. He tells us he likes it too. Weighs 240 when he's clean.

We think of him as a punt return specialist or defensive tackle, depending on what he's been shooting. Has big advantage in that he'll never reach retirement age.

LOUIS ROTHSCHILE: Great moves to the outside. Always a threat to go deep. Set records that will never be broken at Barnard. Can be used either as split end or on the flank. So far, we're the only people interested, which says a great deal for our scout's technique.

★ ★ ★

In conclusion, let me say we're satisfied with last year's draft and we'll be equally satisfied with this year's. We are, as you know, building for the future, just as we were in the past. We always get the people we're looking for.

And if we don't get them, we get what we deserve.

Vintage Juice
1864...and 2003

O. J. Simpson smashed Jim Brown's season rushing record of 1,863 yards as the Bills beat the Jets, but there was a lot more to come

"Hey, man," a Shea Stadium functionary confided to a Buffalo Bill on the sidelines at last Sunday's Bills-Jets game, "the Juice still needs three yards."

"Four," said the Bill, brushing aside the impertinence.

On the next play, with four minutes and 26 seconds remaining in the first quarter, O. J. Simpson gratefully accepted blocks from the left side of his line and churned through the snow for six yards to break Jim Brown's 10-year-old National Football League single season rushing record of 1,863 yards. As befits an occasion of such historic moment, Referee Bob Frederic stopped the game and ceremoniously returned to Simpson the ball he had carried seconds before, whereupon the Juice toted it to the sidelines for safekeeping while most of the 47,750 shivering fans rose to applaud.

Simpson's teammates seemed curiously unmoved, however. They dutifully clapped him on the shoulder pads and noisily extolled him "Way to go, Juice"—but there was little pizzazz in the celebration. It was obvious then that they were looking beyond this achievement to others just ahead.

"More, Juice, more," they chanted as Simpson jogged back to the huddle in his lazy-dog style. "Let's get more."

There was much more. And when, with 5:56 remaining in the game, Simpson burst over left guard for seven yards to the New York 13-yard line, the Bills stormed onto the field and hoisted him to their shoulders in a scene reminiscent of an old Jack Oakie picture. For now the Juice had done it: he had surpassed a hitherto unthinkable distance—2,000 yards—and he had triumphantly closed out a season unparalleled in the history of professional football. There was no need for more.

In this game alone, Simpson had exceeded the legendary Jim Brown's records not only for yardage gained, but for most carries in a season. He surpassed Brown's 305 carries on the same day he surpassed his 1,863 yards and he finished the season with 332 attempts, an average of nearly 24 a game. He had gained 200 yards for the second game in succession and for the third time in a season, both records, and he had enabled the once derided Bills to become the game's first 3,000-yard rushing team, replacing last year's Miami Dolphins as the NFL's alltime top rushers. Earlier in the year he had set two other records by running for 250 yards against New England and carrying the ball 39 times against Kansas City. Preeminently, though, he became pro football's first 2,000-yard man, a 2,003-yard man, in fact, when statistics were revised after the game that, incidentally, the Bills won 34-14 to close out the season with a 9-5 record, their best in seven years.

What is perhaps most remarkable about Simpson's record spree is that it was made possible by two games played on fields of such Siberian frigidity they were fit only for eluding wolves. It snowed throughout the game the previous Sunday at Buffalo when Simpson gained 219 yards against New England and, if anything, it was snowing even more fiercely in New York City last Sunday when he gained 200 yards. While teammates and foes alike were battling futilely to gain purchase on the frozen tundra, Simpson, a native San Franciscan who played for USC in the tarnished sunlight of Los Angeles, traversed the snowscape as swiftly and as surely as an avenging Cossack.

The Juice is really more than a record-breaking record breaker; he is a swashbuckling runner who calls to mind the derring-do of Hugh McElhenny, Jon Arnett, Willie Galimore and Gale Sayers. The 228-pound Brown, who retired in 1966 after nine seasons with the Cleveland Browns to pursue cinematic immortality, was a punishing runner with breakaway speed. Simpson, while no wraith at 212, is the sort of escape artist beloved by fans.

"O. J. senses tacklers," says Houston Oiler Linebacker Dick Cunningham, a former teammate. "He makes cuts that are uncanny. It's almost like the guy coming up behind him is yelling, 'Here I come. You better go the other way.'"

Or perhaps he is, as Hall-of-Famer McElhenny once saw himself, "like a little kid walking down the middle of the street after a scary movie. He can't see anything in the shadows, but he knows something's there that he'd better get away from."

Simpson admits to such sensitivity. No matter how low the temperatures—and they can be cruelly low in Buffalo—he always wears short-sleeved jerseys, exposing bare arms. "I can feel the tacklers better that way," he says. "I can feel their touch, and in a football game I just don't want to be touched. The more I feel that way the better game I play."

He is hardly an untouchable socially. In contrast to the frequently surly Brown, he is relentlessly congenial. And, if that were not enough, he also seems genuinely humble.

The Jet publicity people, anticipating the record onslaught, had set aside a special interview room for Simpson after Sunday's game, where he could preside with Kissingerian imperiousness over the press corps. Simpson entered this chamber with his entire offensive team in tow. "These," quoth he, "are the cats who did the job all year long." And he introduced them all—Wide Receiver J. D. Hill; Flanker Bob Chandler; Tight End Paul Seymour; Tackles Dave Foley and Don Green; Guards Reggie McKenzie ("My main man") and Joe DeLamielleure; Center Mike Montler; Quarterback Joe Ferguson and Fullback Jim Braxton.

"O. J. gives credit where credit is due," said Ferguson, a rookie whose unfamiliarity with NFL defenses hampered the Bills' passing game, permitting opponents to stack their defenses, albeit unsuccessfully, against the Juice's flow. "He's helped me on the field and off. Nobody here is jealous of him. He hasn't got an enemy in the world. All of us wanted to see him get the yardage."

"A record is a collective thing, anyway," says McKenzie, echoing the sentiments of the runner he blocks for. "I'm just thankful to be on the offensive line that broke Jim Brown's record."

Simpson himself is not convinced the record is etched in granite. When asked after the game if he thought 2,003 yards would last, he commented quickly, "No, someone will come along and break it, but I hope to stay in the league until these guys [his offensive line] get so old no young back can get behind them to break my record."

The pressure of record-breaking may have reached him this past week. He refused to accept telephone calls at his New York hotel and protested mildly when photographers hounded him during the game. "Look, man, I can't do that here. C'mon now, no pictures now."

Throughout the season, O. J. had fought to banish the accumulating figures from his mind, even to banish the thought of Jim Brown. There is a peril, he discovered, in keeping tabs on oneself.

"If you think about how much you're gaining," he said recently, "you're not thinking about winning the game. Actually, people are always asking me what I'm thinking about when I'm running. The answer is nothing. Or at least it used to be. But when you get close to a record, you think to yourself, 'If I'm this close, I might as well get it.'

"But I still try not to keep track. Once during a game I heard the guy on the P.A. system announce that 'O. J. Simpson had such and such yards.' It scared me. I went down to the end of the bench and just batted myself in the ears, trying to get it all out of my head. Football is a team game. You can't be thinking about these other things."

It is unlikely, however, that "these other things" escaped Simpson's attention last Sunday. They were definitely on the minds of his teammates, who continually exhorted each other in the bitter cold to "open it up, open it up for the Juice."

Simpson steadfastly avoided such chatter. Huddled in his parka, he sat mostly in solitude on the bench, occasionally exchanging views on blocking assignments with Braxton or Hill, avoiding always the obvious.

But even he gave way to the occasion when Ferguson leaped high after first examining the yard markers to make certain that his friend and teammate had exceeded 2,000 yards. Hoisted aloft by his pals, Simpson raised his left fist in triumph. It was over, and he was through for the day and for the season.

There were no characteristic Simpson long-gainers in this game, his lengthiest run being a 30-yarder on the second play from scrimmage. The nearest he came to bursting free was on a patented sweep of right end in the third quarter. He seemed to be on his way down the snow-packed sideline when he was finally hemmed in by the Jets secondary after a 25-yard gain. It was one of three runs he had during the day of more than 20 yards. Against New England the week before, he had broken loose on a magnificent, snow-churning 71-yard dash. This day he was more workmanlike, more Brownlike.

There are similarities between the game's two supreme rushers, Simpson wears Brown's number, 32, and, like the older man, aspires to a show-business career when his playing days are over.

"Actors have an air about them that athletes don't have," O. J. said the other day, looking decidedly untheatrical in his USC warmup jacket. "You know how people look at Jim. He's that tough guy beating up on everybody, throwing women out windows and shooting up all those people in movies. Really, he's a good guy. But he has a very forceful way about him and people keep their distance. With me, well. . . .

"But it's a real trip being somebody else. I've done a few things in the off-season and I have my broadcasting with ABC television. When I was at SC, I used to work in the studios and I'd watch some of those directors. I think I learned a lot, a lot of technique. I want to play at least two more seasons, until I'm 28. In two more years I'll be financially able to do what I want to do, even if it's nothing. Of course, if we're close to the Big One, I'll want to be there."

Brown, who performed in the pre-Super Bowl era, retired when he still had playing time left, but Simpson insists the actor has never influenced him in anything concerning his affairs. They are friends of a sort, near neighbors in Los Angeles and Simpson occassionally plays basketball at Brown's house. They will talk sports, "although never business," says O. J., "business being football."

Brown is under the impression he first met the man who broke his records when Simpson was an All-America and a Heisman Trophy winner at USC in the late '60s. But Simpson recalls an earlier meeting.

"I really first met him when I was just a kid in San Francisco. It was after a 49er game—I was a big fan of McElhenny and Joe Perry —and a bunch of us had gone across the street from Kezar Stadium to an ice cream parlor where we hung out after games. We were just messing around in there when who should walk in but Mr. Jim Brown himself.

"Well, you know how kids are. We started fooling around, mumbling things, and finally I just walked right up to him and said, 'Mr. Brown, someday I'm going to break all your records, wait and see.' I know it sounds unbelievable now, but I was just kidding around.

"Brown hardly looked at me. He just kind of walked away smiling. Now that we've gotten to know each other, I felt I could ask him if he remembered that time. Naturally, he didn't remember it at all. Why should he? Just some dumb kid."

Mr. Brown might have occasion to remember it now.

The Legend of Squirmin' Herman

The University of San Francisco and St. Mary's College will play a game of football Sunday in Kezar Stadium.

What's that?

Indeed, it does seem a bit strange, if not outright anachronistic. St. Mary's, the erstwhile Galloping Gaels, and USF, the onetime Dons, haven't met on a football field since 1950.

St. Mary's quit football after that season—they were trounced by USF, 33 to 7. And USF fielded only one more team, that being the finest college football team this area may ever see. The 1951 Dons, some may recall, had Ollie Matson, Ed Brown, Gino Marchetti, Bob St. Clair and Burl Toler, to name only a few.

★ ★ ★

As for St. Mary's—well, local people just puddle up recalling those old Slip Madigan teams in the screwy uniforms that annually thumped all the other Catholic schools and took what seemed like a month's vacation traveling to New York to meet Fordham in the Polo Grounds.

St. Mary's, USF and Santa Clara were all football schools in those cynical days. Soon the tail began wagging the dog, and it became apparent that either the teams or the schools would have to go. The teams went; the schools have become prosperous and respectable, if maybe a bit duller.

One can only admire the way the game has been restored to these honored institutions. Now they play it for fun—which, gentlemen, is always the way college football should have been played.

★ ★ ★

But in retrospect, those old days do seem fun. Everything, for that matter, seems fun in retrospect—with the possible exception of basic training.

And somehow I feel it incumbent upon me to dredge up some-

171

thing from the past. Or as Mike Carey, the USF sports information director put it: "Since the USF-St. Mary's traditional battle was at its peak when you were in your college hey-day, you probably have a rich background with regard to the game and rivalry."

Actually, there was nothing rich about me in that hey-day. And despite everything, only one name pops to mind, and it has nothing to do with my college hey-day, for the man in question left St. Mary's a year before I entered college.

He would be, of course, Herman Wedemeyer—"Squirmin' Herman," "Hula-hips Herman," the leader of the Whiz Kids.

★ ★ ★

Herman Wedemeyer certainly isn't the best halfback ever to play college ball in this area.

But his timing was marvelous, and the combination of his Hawaiian ancestry and truly remarkable versatility captured the fancy of an entire nation of football freaks. Grantland Rice, the George Washington of sportswriting, was so overwhelmed by Herman's heroics he selected him the outstanding football player of 1945.

I first saw "Wedey" play as a freshman for a virtually all-freshman St. Mary's team against California in 1943. He intercepted a pass one-handed and weaved through an army of lousy wartime tacklers. It was spectacular.

He was always spectacular. As a freshman, he threw the touchdown pass that tied the Shrine game on New Year's Day of 1944. He came back to St. Mary's after a year of Navy and Merchant Marine duty in 1945 and started all over again. His punt against Cal that year hit the flag on the goal line.

★ ★ ★

In the Sugar Bowl, he ran 25 yards, then lateraled to a guard, who scored the touchdown, thanks to Wedey's block. He was a boxer, a par golfer, a .300 hitter in baseball. He was precisely what a war-woozy public needed.

At 172 pounds, he was too small to be much good as a pro. And he wasn't. For that matter, he was almost a has-been by his senior season.

But those of us who saw him do his inimitable thing will never, ever forget him.

Affairs of the Heart

Persons of a certain age and regional orientation should be forgiven if they persist in regarding the World Series as more of an auditory than a visual experience. Television did not catch them in their formative years; they first *saw* the World Series through the eyes of a radio announcer. The Series was listened to at home, in the back seat of autos, among a cheering crowd clustered outside a small-town appliance store or record shop.

The Series was seen only in the mind's eye, but there the figures grew much larger than they ever would on the small screen. People of this vintage might see the Series as personal fantasy. The romance of baseball, of all sport, is in its capacity for stirring fantasy. We are never too old or too bothered to see ourselves wrapping up a World Series victory with a homer in the final inning of the seventh game.

The game and the players may change but, through the generations, the fans never do. Their hopes rise and fall with the fortunes of their team. The World Series is a sporting event that is both common and exceptional; it is neither as pompous nor as tense as, say, a Super Bowl or a heavyweight championship fight. Baseball is

173

an earthier attraction. And yet it remains a game of gathering tension, and nowhere is this element better demonstrated than in the Series, where nothing that happens is meaningless. Finally, there is the matter of tradition. The World Series has been with us so long that there can be but few among us who can recall a time when it did not exist.

As a Californian, I first thought of the Series as a rare spectacle that sometimes occurred in such exotic places as St. Louis or Detroit, but mainly in New York City, where a San Franciscan was gallantly upholding his own city's tradition of baseball excellence. He was the Yankee Clipper, Joltin' Joe DiMaggio. "Joltin' Joe. . . ." There was a song by that name, and you could hear it, during its brief tenancy on the charts, as you strolled by the radio stores on your way home from school. What was it the man had done to merit a hit swing tune of his own? The lyrics gave few clues, and, out of fear of appearing misinformed in this most important area of juvenile scholarship, I observed a tactical silence, believing that in time the source of Joltin' Joe's magic would somehow be revealed to me. He seemed a hero out of all proportion, one who even clouded the memory of the baseball player we had all heard about, Babe Ruth.

The radio finally explained it: DiMaggio was getting a hit every day that summer of 1941. Nobody, not even Ruth, had done that. Joltin' Joe, the Yankee Clipper, could do everything else, too. He could hit home runs and run down the longest, hardest-hit fly balls. Best of all, he was one of us, a local boy.

The World Series that year was the first I paid much attention to. I was aware, if only dimly, that the Dodgers had won a dramatic victory in their league and that Brooklyn was an unusual place full of odd-looking people speaking a nearly unintelligible patois. It was a team and a place that seemed to seize the public that year. Such native expressions as "dem Bums," "dese" and "dose" and "it's fa da boids" were in vogue, even in San Francisco. The Dodgers were ragtag, dead-end-kid miracle workers. The Yankees were regal, the Dodgers were the canaille at the barricades. A natural inclination now would be to identify with the rabble, but then, inflamed by costume dramas, I equated the Yankees with the British Square confronting screaming hordes of barbarous tribesmen. The Yankees would teach the filthy heathen a lesson.

They did, in five games. The pivotal game was the fourth, in which the Dodgers were leading 4-3 with two out in the ninth. A win would tie the Series and possibly swing the momentum to Brooklyn. The game seemed actually won when Tommy Henrich struck out for what should have been the last out. But Providence intervened. Dodger Catcher Mickey Owen let the ball get by him, Henrich reached first safely, and the next hitter—who else but Joltin' Joe—singled to keep the strange rally alive. The Yankees went on to score four times and effectively clinch the Series. I heard the ninth inning in the back seat of a car—my great aunt's Studebaker, as I recall—and for the first time in my life I advised a woman to kindly shush while I listened to a baseball game. It would not be the last.

Television created new habits in dealing with the World Series. Now the games could be seen at home, in barrooms, at private clubs or, if one was fortunate enough to be employed by a newspaper, in the office. Before the weekday games became night games, playing hooky from the job was a common occurrence in the early weeks of October.

I did not see a World Series game in person until 1962, when my former heroes, the Yankees, now Joltin' Joeless but with Maris and Mantle, came West to play the Giants. It is a pleasure to recall, after this past season when the Giants were almost totally rejected by the community, how affectionately the team was regarded in 1962. The A's would not arrive to carve up the market for another six years, so the Giants had the only game in town. They drew 1,592,594 that year in a considerably smaller (by 15,000 seats) and even windier unenclosed Candlestick Park. It was also the year of the transistor radio, a device affixed to the ear of seemingly every other passerby. The late Russ Hodges' trademark exclamation, "Bye-Bye Baby," was heard in the finest Post Street shops, in the meanest Mission Street taverns and even, as an occasional soprano would complain, in the opera house. The Giants owned the town, and when they won the pennant, champagne flowed in the streets.

My newspaper had assigned me to do "color stories" during the Series games, a duty I perceived as seeking out people in funny hats. The job had two drawbacks: 1) I had no fixed seat in the sold-out ballpark, and 2) if I were to perform with my legendary assiduity, I would not see much of the games. I compromised by finding my oddballs before the games, then watching every inning while seated on the concrete steps of the stadium aisles.

The Series was thrilling enough, but disappointing. The vicious Willie McCovey line drive that would have scored Matty Alou and

Willie Mays with the winning runs in the seventh game was caught by Bobby Richardson somewhere near second base. It was over just like that. I was numb in spirit and in the seat of the pants on my concrete perch. There was a kind of double anticlimax. The Giants had lost and I had seen the Series, if under circumstances far from ideal. What was there left to do now? Become President? Write the Great American Novel? Escape to Tahiti? That is the trouble with experience; it ruins anticipation.

How much more rewarding, in fact, was that Series heard from the back seat of a Studebaker, my first serious meeting with Joltin' Joe. We were to meet again years later. He and I were both patrons of a restaurant operated by Joe's close friend, Reno Barsocchini. DiMaggio would sit silently at one end of the bar, I noisily at the other. He is a private man, and in Reno's that privacy was strictly enforced. Five years ago Reno gave a party for DiMaggio on the occasion of his 56th birthday and the 29th anniversary of his 56-game hitting streak. It was something of an honor to be invited, since the majority of the guests were DiMaggio's old friends from Fisherman's Wharf. It was what DiMaggio enjoyed most, a private party. I was seated across from a man I shall call Charlie, because for the life of me I cannot remember his name. He had been a left-handed pitcher in DiMaggio's playground days, and he, too, was apologetic about being there. "I haven't seen the Clipper [they all called him the Clipper] much since we were kids," said Charlie. "I didn't think he'd remember me."

DiMaggio gave no formal speech. He simply greeted his friends, recalled old times, referred to a few of the guests by name. Finally he spotted Charlie. "Hey, there's Charlie," DiMaggio called out. "Now Charlie here was as fine a young lefthander as I ever saw. Never could understand why he didn't make it to the bigs."

Charlie was flabbergasted. He looked as if he might cry. "Didya hear what the Clipper had to say about me?"

Twenty-nine years had passed since he first held me in his thrall with his hitting streak and his World Series heroics, but I knew then I had never been wrong about Joltin' Joe DiMaggio.

He Was Pappy
To Us All

PAPPY!

Now there's a name for a football coach, implying as it does a kind of benevolent paternalism. A Pappy coach would be a man of some girth, with gray hair and a deep, commanding but gentle voice. He wouldn't be a bit like the lean, hard, intense young technicians who now seem to coach the game.

Instead, he'd be another Lynn O. (Pappy) Waldorf. He would be except there's only one Pappy Waldorf.

Pappy himself, in all of his considerable flesh, indulged happily in what our Donovan Bess properly called "an orgy of nostalgia" at the Shanty Malone testimonial last weekend.

Pappy has always been something of a night person. "Sleep," he once said, "seems to me a waste of valuable time, and I resist it." So he was in his element at the Malone bash.

★　★　★

He was also in the company of many who once played football for him at the University of California in the glory days when the Rose Bowl game seemed a part of the regular season.

Pappy's teams of the late forties may well have been the best ever to represent the university, not that that means so much anymore. But the game was taken seriously at Cal 20 years ago, and the biggest man on campus in every respect was Pappy Waldorf.

The university had fielded such a dismal team in the last pre-Pappy year, 1946, that the student rooters set about dismantling the stadium after a mediocre Stanford team had won the Big Game, 25 to 6.

★　★　★

Pappy came west to the rescue from Northwestern, where he had coached with distinction if not always with success. He had developed a number of outstanding players at the midwestern school,

177

among them Otto Graham. But no one in his right mind could see any way for him to salvage much from the wreckage of the Cal team.

No one, that is, except Pappy. The team, he said, was "a sleeping giant."

The beast awoke in Pappy's first season, winning every game except the one with USC. This single omission was quickly corrected and Cal went undefeated and untied in 1948 and 1949, losing only in the Rose Bowl. In 1950, a tie with Stanford was the only blemish on the record—that and yet another loss in the Bowl game.

Remember that Cal had won only one undisputed conference championship since Andy Smith departed in the 1920s. Suddenly, it had won three in succession. It is doubtful if the conference had ever been so completely dominated by one football team.

★ ★ ★

Waldorf would be the first to admit he had the "horses." Consider Jackie Jensen, Rod Franz, Jack Swaner, Jim Monachino, Pete Schabarum, Johnny Olszewski, Les Richter, Bob Celeri . . . Giants all.

The last really outstanding player Pappy was to develop was Joe Kapp, who as a sophomore 13 years ago led Cal to a 20-18 win over Stanford in Pappy's last Big Game.

"People get tired of seeing the same old faces," he said, and retired to join the 49ers as director of player personnel, a euphemism for head scout.

★ ★ ★

But he was back with the old crowd at Shanty's party, and at 66, he looks and sounds just the same. One of his old players reminded him that he once popped off the bench to report to the coach while licking an ice cream bar.

"You told me to sit down," he reminded Waldorf.

"I'd have sent you in," said Pappy in that parental basso profundo, "if that bar had been fresh. But you'd eaten half way through it so I figured you were out of shape."

Pappy!

A Football Odyssey

*In which the writer travels from Baton Rouge to
Norman to Ann Arbor in 48 hours to watch three
college games and recapture his youth*

Time is at its cruelest when it diminishes remembered things.
Only memory adds stature to the past, for nothing seen again is
ever so formidable. But how easily deceived we are by the mirror of
the mind.

In memory, the school building is a medieval fortress, with laby-
rinthine corridors and enormous rooms presided over by impatient
giantesses. For those of us who in childhood moved from town to
town and school to school—doomed forever, we feared, to dwell in
the special limbo reserved for "the new kid"—a first day in school
was the stuff of recurrent nightmares. Familiarity soon shrinks
classmates, even teachers, to size, but the school, scene of so many
embarrassments, triumphs and disasters, remains in memory a

gigantic place, an Elsinore on dark days, a Camelot on bright ones. Seen today, however, the school building is absurdly small, scarcely more than a large house, a sad, gray place occupied by tiny strangers.

The hometown undergoes an even more curious metamorphosis. In fact, it will have grown larger. There will be newer and taller buildings, sprawling shopping centers, rambling subdivisions, broader streets, even suburbs. But it will never be as big as it once was when its three-story buildings reached to the heavens, towering above the heads of children.

Much the same transformation takes place within ourselves: outwardly, we are larger, but there has been shrinkage inside. Our possibilities become limited, our vision narrowed, our imaginations, once boundless, restricted by the barriers of harsh reality. It is not only the world that grows smaller with each passing day; so do we.

Reflections such as these may be triggered by the most trivial of happenings, the least consequential encounters. Mine came after a football weekend, a "Big Game" odyssey that took me to Louisiana, Oklahoma and Michigan. The cities, the stadiums, the people were all strange to me, but the circumstances were hauntingly familiar, for there was a time when football games and football stadiums seemed so much bigger. Of course, they *are* big. A good-sized stadium can accommodate the population of a small city; its value, once measured in thousands of dollars, now can exceed a hundred million. And yet, stadiums, too, have undergone the melancholy process of diminution.

Each of us in his time has his own stadium. Mine was the University of California Memorial Stadium in Berkeley. Seating nearly 80,000, it is certainly no smaller now than it was three decades ago or even when it was completed in 1923 as a monument to the soldiers of World War I. But it can never be for me what it was when I first entered it as a nine-year-old, marching with mock solemnity in the traffic boy platoon toward the section reserved for our gang in the south end zone. To me, then, it seemed to be the biggest thing I had ever seen. Never had so many people been assembled in one place; never had so many voices been raised at once; never had I been made to feel so small. The Cal players, who were then as, regrettably, they are now, of quite ordinary proportions, seemed Brobdingnagian. It was, you will note, "Cal" then, never "Berkeley," as it has become today. To the children of that

Berkeley long ago, there was but one real university, and that was the one up on the hill. Oh yes, that and something called Stanford.

The Cal Marching Band would rehearse Saturday mornings, then march quick-step to the giant stadium, trailed by us town boys, captives of those uniformed pied pipers. We sprinted to the campus at the first drumbeat, a sound fully as exciting as the final school bell in May. Since we either sneaked in or entered for free in the traffic boy brigade, we never paid for a game. And we rarely missed one. There was but one day of the week—Saturday. Though I would move from Berkeley several times as a boy, those golden Saturdays would stay with me forever. It was all so big.

I cannot say precisely when it was that I lost interest in college football. It was certainly not while I was an undergraduate—a "Cal man" at last—and not immediately after I returned to the Bay Area from military service. No, I would say my interest simply eroded. As a very young man, I had decided to put aside childish things in the false belief that abandoning the past gave certain entry into the promising future. College football seemed to me then a mindless activity pursued only by schoolchildren and incurable Old Blues who were incapable of severing the academic umbilical cord. I was still a football fan, but my team now was the San Francisco 49ers. Berkeley was behind me. That door was closed. You can't go home again.

Then time played another trick. As I grew older and the distance lengthened between the undergraduate me and the supposed man of affairs, I felt a compulsion to close the gap, to rediscover what I had been, to look again at a past that could not be abandoned. I was no longer a stranger in the big stadium on the hill.

It is perhaps the essence of college football, then, that for so many of its followers it should represent a journey through time nearly lost. The past can never truly be recaptured, only sought. The pieces will always be too small to fit old conceptions.

But the college game does at least offer an illusion of youth. The drums beat again. The stadiums seem smaller, the players are too young, but the experience of time renewed persists. The boys follow the band again. . . .

As I have suggested, mine was no ordinary college football weekend; traveling helter-skelter across the midlands, I saw in person, not on the television screen, three games in 48 hours, each of which determined a conference championship. The six teams involved were all ranked in the Top 10 nationally. Their combined

record was a remarkable 53 wins, two ties and a single loss. Four of
the six were undefeated and untied entering these climactic games.
And since each of these match-ups was "a traditional," feelings ran
extraordinarily high in the communities where they were played.
The fans I met along the way were not the people I once knew. But
they shared in common the search. And what could it possibly
matter that they were not actually certain what it was they were
looking for?

ALABAMA CRIMSON TIDE 21
LSU TIGERS 7

Ben and Wellington, two round-faced, bespectacled middle-aged
men, a bit plump, a bit tired but dead game, sit at the curve of the
bar near the pool in Baton Rouge's Bellemont Motor Hotel. They
are removed by only a few feet from the bar's main action, which
happens to be an animated conversation involving two former Alabama players, Johnny Musso and Steve Bisceglia, several 'Bama
assistant coaches and some other in-group types. They are served
by a plump blonde bartendress who in the pale light behind the bar
looks more attractive than she probably is. There is much laughter,
much reminiscing, some flirting.

Ben and Wellington are at the periphery of the inner circle; indeed, they might as well be in Tuscaloosa for the notice paid them
by the others. They return this inattention with affection, laughing
loudly at the eavesdropped anecdotes, joining in from a safe
distance, talking scarcely at all to each other. The pleasures they
gain from this evening will be vicarious.

"Drove seven hours getting here for the Big One tomorrow,"
says Wellington during a slight lull in the main coversation.

"Welly and I never miss a 'Bama game," says Ben.

The stars of the evening are now joking about Musso's new
career in Canadian professional football. "Get my friend here a
Canadian Club," Bisceglia instructs the bartendress. "That's all
they let him drink now."

Ben and Welly chuckle at this one, nodding at each other conspi-
ratorially. They knew Bisceglia had a reputation for wit. He was
obviously under way now.

A group of tall, broad-shouldered young men, four blacks, one
white, obviously football players, step tentatively into the bar,
eyes straining against the darkness. One of them, the white youth,
spots the coaches and quickly ushers the others out.

"Now, what d'ya make of that," one of the assistant coaches remarks, chuckling good-old-boy style. "A white boy from Macon, Ga. leading four blacks into a bar. Times do change."

Ben and Wellington agree that times sure do.

Unlike Musso's, Bisceglia's football career ended at Alabama. He now works for his father in the Bisceglia Brothers Wine Co. in Madera, Calif. The Bisceglia wines, he advises his confreres at the bar, are unequaled for quality, particularly the whites.

"Might I suggest our Imperial Chateau D'Or," he says in the manner of a wine steward. "It so happens that I have a bottle in the glove compartment of my car. If you gentlemen will wait just a moment, I'll go get some. Glasses all round, my dear."

Ben and Wellington nudge each other, smiling at Bisceglia's effrontery. They hurriedly quaff their Scotches in anticipation of the elixir from the California valley. Sharing a glass of wine with these men-in-the-know could open a crack in the conversation through which they might slither. In the darkness their round faces fairly glitter.

Bisceglia returns laughing triumphantly and with a flourish pours wine all round. Or nearly all round.

Ben and Wellington, still happy, still dead game, order two more Scotches. On the rocks.

★   ★   ★

The game-day party at Bill and Jane LeBlanc's sprawling, Southwest-ranch-style house in the Old Goodwood section of Baton Rouge has the feel, despite the landlocked surroundings, of a bon voyage celebration. There is, in fact, a vessel anchored in the LeBlanc driveway—a Blue Bird Wanderlodge mobile home—and the dozen or more of us who will be her passengers are toasting our impending departure in the LeBlanc's lavish bar.

The nautical analogy is not inappropriate, for the Wanderlodge *is* a species of terrestrial yacht. She and scores of sister craft will dock outside Louisiana State's Tiger Stadium this day in berths reserved for them in the parking lot. And like yacht club toffs, the mobile home skippers will hobnob in the docking area, chattering not only about LSU football but about the various idiosyncrasies of their vehicles.

"Damn generator hasn't worked all week. . . ."

"Here, Bill, let me have a look-see. Same thing happened to my Winnebago. . . ."

LeBlanc, LSU, class of 1940, is a balding, long-faced Baton

Rouge businessman of many trades—real estate development, contracting, plumbing—who, though unfailingly courteous, betrays certain xenophobic suspicions during the football season. There is always the dark possibility, however remote, that some auslander may not regard LSU football as the ultimate art form.

"Ah wasn't too sure about you at fust . . . but ah think we'll get along just fine from now on. Glad you're interested in the Tigahs. . . ."

LeBlanc's reverence for his alma mater is untainted by logic, reason or maturity. Louisiana State in the '30s seemed wholly the creation of Huey Long, the state's demagogic governor and United States Senator. The Kingfish, as he was not always affectionately known, pumped state funds into the campus coffers, personally ruled on administrators, even faculty members, led the Tiger band at halftime and freely proferred unwanted counsel to the various football coaches he helped hire and fire. Long saw LSU as the country-cousin antagonist of the city-slick, snobbish private school, Tulane. LSU was Long's baby; for the Cajuns from the bayous it represented freedom from poverty. The country youths who got their education at LSU in this time remain eternally grateful. Their devotion to the Old School is unshakable; a Yalie's allegiance to Eli is, by comparison, tenuous, even frivolous.

LeBlanc's home is a reflection of his own fidelity. A nearly life-size plywood replica of the LSU Tiger, festooned with crepe streamers of purple and gold, hangs above and to the right of the living room fireplace. A stuffed tiger doll, also nearly life-size, stands guard before the couch. On the bar there is a photograph of Mike III, the official team mascot, who growls portentously before each home game. Near Mike there is a cartoon of an LSU tiger suckling at the teats of an Arkansas Razorback. A ceramic tiger lurks in the grass alongside the swimming pool in the backyard. And in the LeBlanc bathrooms, guests scrub with bars of soap on which have been carved tiny, grinning tigers. It is impossible to wash one's hands of the imagery.

★   ★   ★

Crews LeBlanc, Bill's 23-year-old son, is at the helm of the Wanderlodge, and brother Doug, 21, is on the public-address microphone as the football party clambers aboard, plastic glasses in hand. Recorded broadcasts of great moments in the history of LSU football are played on the speaker system. Memories are warmed by hysterical accounts of Billy Cannon's game-winning 89-yard punt return against Mississippi in 1959 or of Bert Jones' last-second touchdown pass also against Old Miss in 1972. The passengers cheer again these epochal achievements.

Doug LeBlanc interrupts the nostalgic broadcast. "As is traditional on these occasions," he announces as the Wanderlodge bounces off the driveway onto the shaded street, "we will begin our trip with a prayer. Today's prayer will be rendered by United States Senator J. Bennett Johnston Jr. Senator Johnston. . . ."

The Senator, a Democrat, rises unsteadily to his feet as the big mobile home lurches down the street.

First off, he suggests, the Lord should see to it that the Wanderlodge safely negotiates the journey to the stadium parking lot. Once the game begins, He should do everything in His power to protect players on both sides from serious injury. Finally, and for this Johnston disqualifies himself as an objective beseecher, He should assure that, in the inevitable victory, the LSU fans and players behave as "good winners." Amen.

"The bar," says Doug, regaining the microphone, "is now officially open."

★ ★ ★

We are a cheerful, if diverse, company of travelers, united presumably by our allegiance to LSU football. Young and old alike, we will root fervently for the Tigers. The Southern young are surprisingly friendly with and respectful of their elders. They chat with them as enlisted men permitted a fling in the Officers' Club. And they seem much less likely to fly the family coop than their contemporaries in the rebellious North. The LeBlanc boys obviously respect their father as the captain of his ship, the Wanderlodge.

"Ah'd like you to meet a friend of mahn," LeBlanc says, introducing a round, pink man with hair the color of twilight. "This is Dr. F. P. Bordelon. The F. P. stands for 'full of penicillin.'"

"That's right," Dr. Bordelon says, acknowledging the introduction. "Ah'm a G. P., general practitioner. Ah give my patients penicillin. If they're allergic to it, ah recommend another physician."

Dr. Bordelon is attired for the game in a purple jacket, purple and gold tie, yellow shirt and flannel slacks that, when hiked up, reveal purple and gold socks with LSU embroidered on them in gold. His underwear, he discretely implies, is similarly adorned.

"Ah'm just a red-headed Cajun," he says proudly. "And don't call me fat. Ah'm not fat. Ah'm just too short for my width."

He is standing outside the Wanderlodge now amid the pregame

hubbub. The stadium rises like a doge's palace in the setting sun. This will be a twilight game. It is warm, in the high 60s, and Dr. Bordelon's forehead is moist.

"Ah tell ya, ah owe this place an awful lot. Ah tell mah own children ah don't care where they go to school as long as it's LSU. Going to these games is a little like going home again. Football may be a lil' different heah in the South. It's a fashion show, a parade, all those parties, these won'ful people. In the North, it may be just a game. Heah, it's a way of life."

★   ★   ★

Tiger Stadium is known in the South as "Death Valley," no reflection, certainly, on its playing surface, which, far from being an arid wasteland, is a lush green lawn of unartificial, real live grass. The sobriquet refers instead to the grisly fate that awaits even the best teams to visit an arena housing patrons so fiercely partisan. Visitors to this Death Valley succumb not to thirst but to earache, for it is THE NOISE that ultimately does them in. Just as Los Angeles baseball fans once applauded themselves for showing up in such great numbers, thereby shattering all existing attendance records, so do Tiger fans raise their voices in tribute to THE NOISE they can make of an evening.

The stadium is acoustically perfect for cacophony. Its seats, which are close to the sidelines, rise sharply above the field so that even a hiccup from the 40th row resounds in the huddle like the report of an artillery piece. And when 68,000 Tiger zealots scream in unison, the effect on even the most placid of quarterbacks is unsettling.

The sound of a thousand rock concerts attends the arrival of the first Tiger player. By the time the entire team has been trotted out, Lindbergh has been feted at Le Bourget, V-J day has been acclaimed in Times Square and Judy Garland has sung *Over the Rainbow* in a comeback appearance at the Palace.

But on this night, Alabama will play with such calculated ferocity that by the final gun THE NOISE has dwindled to a groan. Alabama is LSU's superior in everything, including dress. The Tigers, for whatever reasons of austerity or defective laundry facilities, appear in soiled tearaway jerseys that are mostly tornaway even before the game. With bare midriffs, they resemble so many down-at-the-heels Seventh Avenue streetwalkers. Alabama is crisp and neat in red and white. They subdue the tatterdemalion opposition with minimal exertion.

The alliterative headline the following morning in the Baton Rouge *Morning Advocate* reads: BEAR'S BAMANS BURST BENGALS' BUBBLE.

NOISE notwithstanding.

★   ★   ★

OKLAHOMA SOONERS 27
NEBRASKA CORNHUSKERS 0

From the air, sighted through a thin mauve haze above the flat gray plains, the University of Oklahoma's Owen Field in Norman looks like nothing more than a large bowl of tomato soup. Oklahoma will play its traditional opponent, the University of Nebraska, this day, and though the official colors of the two schools are not identical—Oklahoma is crimson and cream, Nebraska scarlet and cream—in the stadium they are, with only minor gradations in shading, all red.

On the field, Oklahoma wears red jerseys, red helmets and white pants; Nebraska has white helmets, white jerseys and red pants. Supporters of both teams wear red hats, red sweaters, red corsages, red bandannas, even red socks. They wave red bandannas and shake red pompons. And since temperatures are in the 70s and the air is still and moist and spirits are high, they are mostly red-faced.

A large red bus is parked outside the stadium entrance on which, painted boldly in white, is this message: THOUGH YOUR SINS ARE SCARLET, THEY BE WHITE AS SNOW.

For Oklahoma the inscription is apt, even prophetic. Damned by the NCAA for illegal recruiting and declared ineligible, therefore, for postseason games, the scarlet Sooners will soon beat hell out of untainted Nebraska. ON TO THE PROBATION BOWL proclaims a red banner held aloft.

It is a dull and, yes, colorless conquest. There is no noise in quiet Norman, save for that in the stadium, and by LSU aural criteria, there is none there. The game is over almost before it begins. The sinners' triumph is merciless, swift and convincing.

For a rivalry of such consequence, the contest stirs few emotions. The student newspaper, *The Oklahoma Daily*, plays the 10th anniversary of President Kennedy's assassination on Page One; the "Battle of the Big Reds" is merely an inside feature. There is no inspirational march music at halftime. Instead, this period is dedicated to the *oeuvre* of composer-conductor Henry Mancini, who, neatly turned out in sports coat, slacks and porkpie hat, acknowledges the tribute in person. He mounts a stepladder and, teetering precariously there, bows, hat in hand, to his admirers.

The "Boy Scout Stretcher Team" is also applauded this day, though the dreary encounter on the field excites no one to collapse and the stretcher-bearers' role is superfluous. There is also an announcement on the public-address system that the Oklahoma basketball team will play "Yugoslavia" later in the week. Will the Serbo-Croats fare better than the Cornhuskers? The Yugoslavia Reds?

After the game, what seems to be the vast majority of the 60,000 fans assembles at O'Connell's Irish Pub for pitchers of 3.2 beer. The red-jacketed, red-eyed crowd spills out of the roomy pub into the parking lot. Inside, the decor is singularly un-Gaelic. Elk, moose and buffalo trophies stare morosely out from the walls. In one room, films of old Floyd Patterson fights are shown. Floyd Patterson? Can that brooding old pugilist mean anything to this generation? And yet there he is, a lithe, quick figure, the face all apology as he bangs the setups comatose. Students and young alumni watch the combat listlessly.

O'Connell's is crowded, but, like the stadium before it, strangely silent. "We are the best football team in the country," says Larry Killebrew, a young radiologist from Oklahoma City. "But we can't prove it."

It is a sage observation, explaining all. Each Oklahoma victory is a measure of revenge on those who passed judgment on the school, but since winning leads nowhere, it is essentially meaningless. This will be the year of waiting until next year.

"Though your sins are as scarlet, they will be white as snow. . . ."

★ ★ ★

MICHIGAN WOLVERINES 10
OHIO STATE BUCKEYES 10

In the distance, as the motley procession advances on the stadium through the cold mist, you can hear THE SONG:

"Hail! to the victors valiant
Hail! to the conquering heroes,
Hail! Hail! to Michigan. . . ."

It will be played endlessly, for this is the 75th anniversary of its composition, a fight song to end all fight songs, composed in the flush of victory on a train ride back from Chicago.

"Hail! Hail! to Michigan. . . ."

Despite a heavy chill, the dampness and the dense traffic, the multitudes plodding toward the gigantic stadium in Ann Arbor are in high good humor, exchanging japes in their traffic-choked cars, flourishing fanciful signs—SAVE FUEL, BURN WOODY—and singing, singing, singing. They are dressed against the cold and drizzle as if for a masquerade ball. Four men in identical yellow plastic trousers wade through the mud of the golf course near the stadium. They are like Ingmar Bergman creations, ghostly clowns dancing in the mist.

This is clearly football weather, meaning bad. In Baton Rouge and Norman it had been unseasonably warm. Here there is the threat of snow or freezing rain. The stadium rises spectrally in the distance, so massive that not even time can reduce it to mortal proportions. It is nearly as large as when I first saw it 25 years before. Actually, then it had fewer seats. A record crowd of 105,223 will watch this game between two undefeated teams playing for the championship of the Big Ten and the privilege of defending the conference's honor in the Rose Bowl. From the field, the rim of the stadium is lost in the gray skies.

Time does not move swiftly in the Big Ten. Everything seems as it once was. The teams play foot-slogging antediluvian football with line plunges, stout defense and little or no passing. There is a certain majesty to this stubborn resistance to change.

The Michigan Marching Band, playing *its* Big Game, tootles with such dogged vigor that even the players feel compelled to call for silence as the game itself, a match between dinosaurs, begins. THE SONG is cut short in mid-chorus.

"Hail! to the vic . . ."

From the Michigan sidelines, Woody Hayes, the totalitarian Ohio State coach, appears in the mist as a glowering eminence grise, pacing restlessly before his bench, snarling at officials. Michigan's Bo Schembechler, a Hayes protege, is nearly as adept as his master at referee-baiting. He is regarded coldly and without rancor by the objects of his relentless wrath.

The Michigan players on the bench watch dejectedly as Ohio State's Archie Griffin, a rapier of a runner, perforates their defense. When Griffin is finally brought to ground, the Wolverines attack him savagely. Safety Dave Brown chases him through most of the long afternoon, upsetting him when he can with body blocks, necktie tackles and desperate snatches at his clothing. Brown stands panting over the fallen Griffin, his expression betraying the certain fear that he will rise again. Griffin will accumulate 163 yards on 30 carries despite the best efforts of Brown and his fellow defenders.

The Michigan quarterback, Dennis Franklin, is the eye of the hurricane in this stormy game. His brown face is impassive, his mood detached. But with slightly more than two minutes left to play, he lies motionless in the Michigan backfield after completing a short rollout pass. He is helped off the field with the score tied. He clutches his right shoulder but his face is vacant of either suffering or disappointment. He has a broken collarbone, a bad break for him and his school, for though Michigan has tied the conference champion, the Big Ten athletic directors will later vote to send Ohio State to the Rose Bowl rather than permit a team without a starting quarterback to play the Pacific Eight winners. They cannot risk a fifth consecutive loss to the West Coast.

The game ends inconclusively. There is no elation on either bench, although Michigan supporters seem confident that the Rose Bowl will be theirs. Had not Ohio State gone and lost the year before? Is it not someone else's turn?

The band is on the field before the players are off it. False hopes are betrayed with the playing of *California, Here I Come*. Then, as the rooters raise their umbrellas in triumph, the band swings passionately into THE SONG:

"Hail! to the victors valiant,
Hail! to the conquering heroes,
Hail! Hail! to Michigan, the champions of the West. . . ."
It is to be a swan song.

★   ★   ★

The postgame celebrants in the American Legion Hall a block from Michigan Stadium are hardly collegiate. They are men and women of middle years and working-class apparel. They are loud, even boisterous, and in a singing mood. THE SONG comes to them from a venerable jukebox in the cavernous barroom. Recorded by Jan Garber and his orchestra, it is A-1 on the old box.

Two men, both probably in their late 50s, one wearing a raincoat, the other a mackinaw, are watching the USC-UCLA game on one of the television sets above the bar. The telecast followed by about half an hour the end of the Ohio State-Michigan game. These men raced to the hall as quickly as they could in order to get good field position at the bar, for it is assumed the USC-UCLA winner will be Michigan's opponent in the Rose Bowl. The two grizzled viewers do, however, deplore Michigan's inability to gain more than a tie from the Buckeye game. They are inclined to place the blame for this oversight on Franklin, considered by most of the experts to be, with Griffin, the star of the game. Mackinaw and Raincoat do not see it that way. Franklin, they agree, should not be playing quarterback for the simple reason that he is black and, in their view, blacks never make good quarterbacks.

"You don't see any of *them* in the NFL," says Mackinaw.

"That's right," says Raincoat. "No spooks there."

UCLA's quarterbacks, though indisputably white, are having notably less success with USC than Franklin had with the Buckeyes. The two viewers are quick to observe that one of the frustrated signal-callers is Mark Harmon, son of the immortal Tommy, the Michigan football hero of more than three decades ago.

"Saw Tommy play right here many, many times," says Mackinaw, as, with consummate timing, A-1 is played on the jukebox. "Now there was a football player. Don't see his kind anymore."

"How come," inquires Raincoat, "he let his kid go to school out West?"

"Just look," replies Mackinaw, gesturing toward the screen. "It's obvious. He wasn't good enough to play here."

"Hail! Hail! to Michigan. . . ."

★ ★ ★

Harmon? Tommy Harmon? Old 98! Why, he played in my stadium the year I discovered it. Scored four touchdowns against Cal, long runs on three of them. The Cal defense had so much trouble with him that Bud Brennan, a bald real estate salesman, much in his cups that day, staggered out of his seat on the west side of the stadium and, topcoat flailing in the wind, set off after Harmon, who was running, as usual, in the clear. Harmon gently placed a hand on Brennan's bald pate as the realtor lunged for him at the goal line. "What in hell are you doing here?" the All-America halfback asked. Brennan, winded now, managed to mutter an obscenity before the campus police arrived to haul him off. It was a memorable occasion.

Yes, memorable. That's it. A chance remark by two not very likable strangers in a town almost completely foreign to me had initiated a predictable response. College football is a continuum, just as any truly valuable sport is. Everything changes, nothing changes. Harmon *fils* recalls Harmon *pere*. The past, despite the increasing distance we put between it and ourselves, is never far away.

Is this what so many of us find in college football? Do we see something there, if only indistinctly, that survives despite time's powers of diminution?